Women and the University Curriculum

Towards Equality, Democracy and Peace

Edited by
Mary-Louise Kearney and Anne Holden Rønning

Foreword by Attiya Inayatullah

Jessica Kingsley Publishers

UNESCO Publishing

Layout: Inger M Skæveland Carter, Department of English, University of Bergen, Norway

First published in the United Kingdom in 1996 by
Jessica Kingsley Publishers Ltd
116 Pentonville Road, London N1 9JB, England
and 1900 Frost Road, Suite 101, Bristol, PA 19007, U S A

and

The United Nations Educational, Scientific and Cultural Organization,
75700 Paris, France

Copyright © 1996 UNESCO

Library of Congress Cataloging in Publication Data
A CIP catalogue record for this book is available
from the Library of Congress

British Library Cataloguing in Publication Data
A CIP catalogue record for this book is available from the British Library

JKP ISBN 1-85302-399-X
UNESCO ISBN 92-3-103243-7

Printed and Bound in Great Britain by Cromwell Press, Melksham, Wiltshire

This book is due for return on or before the last date shown below.

-9. JAN. 1998

Contents

Foreword

Women and the University Curriculum: Towards Equality, Democracy and Peace is a fitting contribution by UNESCO both to the aims of the fourth World Conference on Women (Beijing, 1995) and to the strategies proposed to advance the condition of women on the eve of the twenty-first century.

UNESCO accords the greatest importance to the role of women graduates who, because of their training, constitute part of a country's skilled human resources and are therefore in a position to make a significant contribution to the process of sustainable human development. They contribute in various ways – as professionals within their chosen domains of expertise, as decision-makers through their influence on policy issues related to social, economic and cultural development and through their participation in family and community life.

Education is thus a principal means to empower women so that they realize their potential. In our world where rapid and radical changes have become common phenomena, citizens and specialists must fully assume their individual and collective responsibilities so that the development process is assured. Higher education, a key factor in capacity-building for each nation, has special reponsibility for humanity's ability to attain the goals of sustainable development and peace. These are the objectives of the United Nations family of which UNESCO is a part.

This publication analyses the gender dimension of the university curriculum. It is intended as a concrete strategy to sensitize today's students to the condition of women in our society. Different disciplines are examined: in some instances, the gender dimension is effectively included; in others, it has struggled for recognition or has yet to be adequately understood and incorporated. At present, we are in a transitional period – much has been achieved in terms of gender equality but many challenges clearly remain.

The authors plead the case in favour of the gender dimension with conviction. Their arguments for its justification and positive impact are impressive. If it is recognized that bold and innovative steps are required for the successful management of social change, then higher education must ensure that knowledge and its applications truly serve humanity. These studies illustrate that the role of women in development can be better understood so as to progress towards the attainment of equality, democracy and peace.

Attiya Inayatullah
Chairperson
UNESCO Executive Board

Women, Higher Education and Development

Mary-Louise Kearney
UNESCO

I. Introduction

The 4th World Conference on Women (Beijing, 1995) chose as its theme "Equality, Development and Peace". These objectives have yet to be attained by many women in the world of today. While the principles of equal opportunity and development are well recognized, it is now agreed that the rhetoric must be matched by concrete strategies which realize these goals.

Over the past 25 years, a great deal has been achieved in terms of sensitizing countries to the particular issues related to the rights of women and to their full participation in society, notably their presence at the decision-making levels. However, much remains to be done as is evidenced by statistics stated in Human Development Report published annually by the United Nations Development Programme:

- 66% of the world's illiterates are women;
- only 33% of women compared to men enrol in higher education in Sub-Saharan Africa;
- their participation in employment is only 50% compared to that of men in developing countries;
- maternal mortality rates remain 15 % higher in the developing world;
- women in certain countries still cannot vote or own property;
- in politics they represent only 10% of the world's parliamentarians;
- national GNPs could rise significantly if women's unpaid work was an official factor in production.

Clearly rapid change must occur and the role of education, notably as an investment in human capital, is an essential aspect of this challenge.

Women in higher education is an area where partnerships have become more significant because different types of expertise can be associated to produce a new synergy which is able to have an enhanced impact in resolving the problems at hand. Hence, the collaboration of UNESCO and the International Federation of University Women (IFUW) is particularly effective in this regard. On the one hand, UNESCO is the agency of the United Nations which covers education, science (including the social sciences), culture and communication. As these are vital forces in the development process in every country, UNESCO has an important contribution to make to global initiatives - such as the Beijing Conference, the World Social Summit (Copenhagen 1990), the International Conference on Population and Development (Cairo 1994), to name but three. On the other hand, IFUW is the NGO which specializes in the issues related to women regarding both their access to and participation in higher education and their contribution as graduates to social development. The commonality of their concerns is thus clear.

The link between the university curriculum and gender issues has always been an important topic but now, given its potential, it merits closer attention. The purpose of this book is to identify whether and how the teaching, training and research functions of higher education sensitize students to the principal questions affecting women and their role in society.

The long-term objective of this exercise merits reflection because it promotes the processes of sustainable human development and peace which are the twin cornerstones of the United Nations system. Today the International Development Strategy (IDS) proposed by the UN advocates investment in human resources as the best way of generating social and economic growth. In the words of the 1994 Human Development Report:

"Human beings are born with certain potential capabilities. The purpose of development is to create an environment in which all people can expand their capabilities and opportunities can be enlarged for both present and future generations. The real foundation of human development is universalism in acknowledging the life claims of everyone."

This view is further reiterated in two major documents, *An Agenda for Development* and *An Agenda for Peace,* published by the UN in 1995. While recognizing that the attainment of these objectives is a complex task, all nations - and their peoples - are called to co-operate to ensure the emergence of a more socially just and conflict-free society. Thus, men and women have equal responsibility in meeting this challenge.

Against this background, renovation of the university curriculum has become one particular way to tackle problems - old and new - through changes in the teaching and learning processes at the grass roots level. However, to do this effectively, several other related areas must be borne in mind:

- firstly, the current climate of **radical change and reform within higher education itself** must be considered in order to situate the issues of curriculum renovation and women's education in context;

- secondly, the **main aims and expected outcomes of the human development process need to be articulated.** The final declaration of the 1995 World Social Summit attested to the concern expressed by all nations for social policy issues. While grave in themselves, these can have particularly serious consequences for women.

Building on these two perspectives, it becomes easier to study the background factors affecting women, their links with higher education, human development and the culture of peace. As a result, new light is cast on the issue of **women's empowerment** and on aspects of their **access to and participation** in higher education, including **discriminatory practices.**

From this basis, the question of curriculum innovation and inclusion of gender issues across various disciplines may be newly defined and better understood. It becomes important to obtain views from specialists representing diverse regions and disciplines. It is also essential to analyse the concept of feminine leadership in the academy since this is a crucial factor affecting women's participation in the decision-making areas of higher education.

II. Challenges facing Higher Education Today

Higher education institutions have, historically, provided their societies with skilled human resources - notably social and economic decision-makers and specialists in all professional fields. And yet, on the eve of the 21st century, higher education is in the midst of profound self-examination in order to determine strategies to provide its traditional contribution in innovative and effective ways.

Today, the capacity-building role of higher education must respond to the challenges of diversified training, while assuring the quality of the expertise produced.

This challenge is due to the complex trends dominating higher education policy-making worldwide of which five are of particular significance:

i.   the continued demand for access which has doubled and even tripled in some countries, necessitating a shift from elite to mass higher education;

ii.   the continued reduction of financial resources and growing accountability measures imposed by governments, some of which have been forced to cut funding by up to 40%;

iii. the maintenance of quality and relevance and the measures required for their assessment. This problem will grow since student numbers could reach 120 million by the year 2050;

iv. the ongoing problem of graduate employment which is forcing a reassessment of academic degrees and diplomas;

v. the growing reality of internationalization in higher education teaching, training and research which promotes the shared creation and transfer of knowledge and know-how and so impacts upon institutional management, curriculum and the profiles of professors and students alike. In this area, higher education is clearly reflecting a new approach to social policy where analysis and formulation must take account of global issues.

Thus, more than ever before, higher education must strive to produce:

• well-educated citizens and professionals;
• sufficient numbers of skilled personnel;
• training which is relevant to diverse contexts and needs;
• expertise which is internationally recognized but directly applicable to local problem-solving (and hence, to the reduction of the Brain Drain).

In this task, all actors of the higher education community - policy-makers, institutional leaders, the professoriate, the student body, scientific and research personnel - have a special responsibility as the contribution of each group is essential.

These phenomena and issues dominate the recent Policy Papers entitled *Higher Education: The Lessons of Experience* and *Higher Education for Change and Development*, prepared respectively by the World Bank and UNESCO.

In essence, the Bank believes that higher education has become too expensive in many countries and that its future costs must be increasingly transferred to its users - the logic being that they will gain from this investment via higher incomes during their working lives. The demand for access should be met through increased diversification and special programmes to cater for disadvantaged social groups, including women, should be introduced.

While concurring with the gravity of present economic conditions and acknowledging the future predictions for graduate employment, UNESCO reiterates the principle of social equity. Those with the requisite entry qualifications should be entitled to higher education. Although other funding will be needed, it is still, principally, the duty of the state to ensure that adequate resources and delivery systems are available. Furthermore, UNESCO's paper focuses on the importance of maintaining quality and relevance which can be achieved if countries adopt a holistic view of higher education. This strives to balance education and training and to attune all types of higher education studies - whether academic or more vocational - to the diverse needs of society as a whole.

Moreover, UNESCO proposes an agenda for pro-active institutions of higher education so that these can learn to manage change efficiently and effectively. In this way, they may satisfy both their funding sources and, at the same time, prove their worth to their communities through the high calibre of the graduates they produce - as citizens and as professionals in various fields.

While these analyses of higher education today may differ, both fully recognize the inherent paradox of doing more with less - quality and relevance cannot be maintained if the human and financial resources provided are ultimately inadequate. This situation is placing immense pressure on all areas of the higher education community - but especially on institutional leaders, the professoriate and the students who are the main clients in the teaching and learning process.

Given the constraints, a holistic approach to national and institutional issues recommends that all partners join forces in the search for a common objective - the enhanced quality and relevance of higher education in a climate of profound change and crisis. Only through such a co-operative effort can positive results perhaps be obtained for all concerned. On the one hand, ongoing dialogue should take place between national policy-makers and institutional leaders. On the other hand, inside institutions, each group should be able to envision its role and contribution to the overall aim of excellence in teaching, training and research. This requires effective interface which results from clear statements of overall mission and individual purpose. Last but not least, solid and cordial relations must be established with society at large, including the economic sector. In this way, the institution may serve its community and its needs - on the national, regional and international scales.

Against this background, two specific aspects related to higher education and women become clearer:

- firstly, **women graduates must be seen as part of the essential human resource base of each country**. As such they have then right to the same access and career opportunities as their male counterparts. Discriminatory practices are not only unjust but a flagrant wastage of valuable expertise which, today, is vital for all nations;

- secondly, to optimize the contribution of all graduates, their training must be of high calibre and of social relevance. In this respect, **curriculum renovation takes on new significance as it must tackle current global problems and their solution at local levels.** Thus, it becomes necessary to examine gender issues as these relate to different disciplines in this particular light.

III. The Challenges of Sustainable Human Development and Peace

Today, the United Nations seeks to promote a vision of the future in which sustainable development and human security are interdependent. Unless this is so, no major goal - peace and democratization, environmental protection, population control, sufficient food production or social integration - can be achieved.

As global problems and conflicts continue to proliferate, humanity is challenged to alter its perspective and redesign its agenda. For this reason, the 1995 World Social Summit - held in the year marking the 50th anniversary of the United Nations - centred its debate for the first time on key elements of social policy, namely **poverty, employment and social marginalization**.

Seven specific outcomes were foreseen:

- revival of the growth process;
- affirmative action for the poor;
- empowerment of marginal and disadvantaged groups;
- targeted employment generation;
- human resource development;
- labour market reforms;
- social security and democratization.

Linking these to UNESCO's field of competence, action for sustainable human development and peace has 9 main targets:

- strengthening of endogenous capacity-building;
- the participation of people in social development, including due respect for human rights, democracy and tolerance;
- recognition of the role of cultural factors in development strategies;
- the promotion of a new vision of employment and work within a broader concept of "active life";
- an improved quality of life for rural populations;

- better environmental awareness;
- more equitable sharing of science and technology;
- ensuring that the communication media serve social development;
- the provision of endogenous skills in social-policy-making, evaluation and management.

How do these principles and strategies relate to women and higher education?

As stated already, higher education is the traditional area for the training of a nation's skilled human resources. Thus, investment in graduates of high calibre but able to practically apply their talents is a top priority for all countries today. Because of this, women who have benefited from higher education can and must influence the social process in every way possible. In carrying our this duty, they reaffirm that all graduates - male and female - have equal responsibility to make a worthwhile contribution in their chosen field of endeavour.

Furthermore, the value of women's contribution to society is still not adequately recognized. In the home, in the workplace, in the community - each of these contexts owes a great deal to the presence and influence of women whose talents can enhance their character, structure and impact on society as a whole. This contribution is unique and must be allowed to flourish.

The gravity of the issues raised at the World Social Summit and the need to replace conflict and aggression by social harmony and progress are fully understood by women through their various roles in society. Thus, their views and recommendations for solutions constitute a crucial voice in the debate.

Because of their multi-faceted contribution to family, community and professional life, women have emerged as vital actors in this search for sustainable human and social development. This could hold the key to our future because it implies the realization of human potential and its productive utilization. It presupposes investment in important sectors of society - education, health and social services as well as in culture as a means of developing the human identity.

All women understand the importance of transmitting spiritual values and the link between these and social harmony. Already the development process has recognized the need to utilize this special wisdom in regions such as Africa and Asia. In the industrialized world, women are urged to take a more active part in the decision-making processes in all areas of their lives. In this way, spiritual values can be promoted at the grass roots level and thus the likelihood of their being adopted on a wider basis is strengthened.

If human development is to play this central role in the achievement of social and economic equity, it must have its roots in the powerful values of freedom, democracy, respect for human rights and tolerance. These and these alone are the valid indicators of real development. Without these, progress based solely on economic wealth and on technological advances will surely founder and end in social disintegration.

Last but not least, gender issues are pertinent for the promotion of a **Culture of Peace.** As this and sustainable human development constitute the overarching goals for UNESCO's 4th Medium Term Plan (1996-2001), these concepts will orient UNESCO's action in the areas of education, science, culture and communication during this period.

Women have a major role to play in building this culture because they can help create a society where discord and unrest are replaced by peace. Moreover, this will be based on a profound comprehension of the very nature of tolerance and the necessity to promote this value in an increasingly multicultural and economically interdependent world.

Higher education also has a role to play in such a culture - but as yet, this has not been explored in sufficient depth. At this level of education, complex issues are analysed - via disciplines such as

Economics, Demography and Sociology. In addition, the moves to develop interdisciplinary studies allow reflection on the causes and on the nature of social change - an area where the Social Sciences are concerned.

Last but not least, a perceived renewal of interest in the Humanities - Literature and Art - as well as in History and Philosophy can be viewed as another avenue to the peace-building process. Through these, students can better appreciate other peoples, their cultures and the complex events which have shaped history in different regions of the world.

If such knowledge can help engender the desired understanding, human attitudes could be significantly changed. As a result, human behaviour may alter for the better - thus allaying the dangers of instability and aggression which have proved to have dire social and economic consequences for all nations.

IV. Women and Higher Education: Key Aspects

Participation in Decision-making
Decision-making attests to the empowerment of the various actors involved. At the present time, far too few women possess this attribute. Education facilitates empowerment which is essential for the participation of women in all aspects of the development process. Furthermore, higher education provides the expertise usually required for the key posts which shape policy in all fields - hence its particular importance for women is obvious.

The increased participation of women in decision-making is probably the domain where urgent action is most required - a fact emphasized in the Beijing Platform of Action. This is because the need for meaningful social change has become crucial. At the end of the 20th Century, the entire sphere of decision-making is in question on account of the gravity of current issues and the failure of leaders to find lasting solutions. Traditional models of leadership are under scrutiny as social problems proliferate and as economic conditions continue to stagnate and decline. The rapid political changes towards democracy which marked the end of the 1980s have not brought the expected climate of world peace, since, in too many regions, ethnic and cultural conflicts continue to exist. Men and women alike are suffering as a result of such issues.

These adverse conditions affect the shaping of social policies in a special way since world leaders are now obliged to seek fresh approaches to local and global problems. Such approaches can draw on innovative experimental practices which have yielded positive results in terms of enhanced social and human development - a goal which will benefit men and women everywhere. The focus must be on the common destiny of humanity which, in an interdependent world, requires knowledge and know-how to survive. To this end, education is perceived as playing an increasingly important part as it ensures that both the realization of human potential and its productive utilization can come about.

In many spheres of life, women are found in subordinate roles. Even in the field of education where they make up the majority of the work force they are less often to be found as heads of departments, universities and research institutions. Too few governments and international agencies have taken steps to promote women to positions of greater responsibility.

Women are particularly poorly represented in parliaments where they can take part in the decision-making at national and international levels. The International Parliamentary Union Report for 1985 showed that during the International Women's Decade the increase in women's representation in parliamentary assemblies was less than 2 per cent. In Norway the number of women cabinet ministers is an encouraging 47 per cent. But women make up only 7.2 per cent of university professors and 3.3 per cent of business corporations. In the Nordic countries, women are held in high esteem and have been successfully elected to parliament - their numbers exceed 30% in the lower houses of parliament in Finland and Denmark, while in Sweden this figure is 38% In contrast, women in developing countries make up less than 10% of elected representatives.

The goals set by the United Nations for increasing the number of women in its Secretariat and agencies have still to be reached. The statistics show a small number of women at the decision making level. In 1991 only four (10%) UN agencies were headed by women.

The small number of women in executive positions is due to their lack of information and to unfavourable selection procedures. Women find it more difficult than men to follow a career which enables them to reach executive status. Since 1990 it seems that women in Eastern Europe have tended to withdraw more from public life and returned to traditional attitudes towards the place of women in society. As a result, when major and far-reaching reforms are being introduced, they are absent from the decision-making process.

The programming of career development has always been difficult for women. The important years for career building are also those of child bearing and their family responsibilities may hinder their career advancement. Women are often excluded from selection because they are less aware than men of the "covert criteria" for appointments to executive positions. Other important barriers to women's participation in decision-making include: (a) family attitudes; (b) alienation from the male culture and continued resistance to women in management position; and (c) inadequate policies and legislation to ensure their participation. At the community level, women are appointed to local committees though there is still a tendency for final decisions to be made by men.

The principal barriers preventing the participation of women in the decision-making arena include: 1) limited access to education, especially higher education; 2) discriminatory appointment and promotion practices; 3) the stresses of dual family and professional roles; 4) family attitudes 5) career interruptions; 6) cultural stereotyping; 7) alienation from the male culture and continued resistance to women in management positions; 8) propagation of the glass ceiling syndrome which privileges covert criteria for advancement; and 9) absence of adequate policies and legislation to ensure the participation of women *(Women in Higher Education Management,*1993)

Given these obstacles, solutions to remedy the exclusion of women lie in a reversal of these trends by means of wider access to education, notably higher education, review of appointment and promotion procedures, provision of legislative and infra-structure support in all professions and of special programmes for women, affirmative action to favour women's access and participation while awaiting a genuine change in attitude towards full gender equality and institutional and governmental support through clear and effective policies which are actually enforced.

Within this perspective, the concept and successful practice of feminine leadership is rapidly coming into sharper focus. More must be known about this phenomenon and the real social progress which it can propel - whatever the context where it may occur. Also, further research on male attitudes to power-sharing is required. At the moment, feminine leadership and its possible benefits constitute a controversial area of the debate in terms of empowerment for women. Some would argue in favour of an equal but clearly specific management style and the espousal of certain values; others would deny any difference, insisting that access to decision-making depends on emulation of male behaviour. However, despite this divergence of opinion, both sides would agree that truly able women leaders have an obligation to assist other competent women.

Participation in Higher Education
Higher education plays a part in national development and this includes the advancement of women. Higher education helps women in two ways. It enables qualified women to become

leaders in society and allows them to become role models for younger girls. University planners, restricted by a lack of resources and by the priority given to basic education, have many obstacles to overcome if they are to provide access to courses, provide the necessary funding and diversify the number of courses available. These tasks have been complicated by the introduction of innovative methods of instruction using global information technologies and by the fact that higher education is international in character and staff tend to be more mobile than in the past.

The fact that there are fewer employment opportunities for women also discourages them from following courses in higher education. Other factors which prevent them from entering universities include: a) early marriage and family responsibilities; b) lack of career guidance; and c) inability to assume personal and professional responsibilities. Women who enter universities tend to follow courses in arts and social sciences for lack of competence in mathematics and science. Women are thus often excluded from senior positions in the field of technology.

At the present time, women remain seriously under-represented at the higher education level and in professional life in general. In contrast, their male counterparts who achieve similar qualifications and experience, generally meet with greater careers success and participate fully in management processes. As a result of this imbalance, women are too absent from the management of social change in general. As long as such under-representation persists, the trained human resources of a country are not being utilized to optimal effect.

The past 20 years have witnessed significant - but not sufficient - enrolment of the female population in higher education. This progress has certainly been due in part to specific strategies which have focused attention on the inequalities to be redressed. UN action has been effective in this regard as policy-makers have been sensitized to the rights of women and to the need to open all levels of education to their greater numbers. A closer analysis of higher education statistics reveals the different nature of the problem in different socio-cultural and economic contexts.

In developing countries, even where female enrolment often made impressive progress during the 1980s, the overall pattern for 1990 shows that women continue to lag behind men:

Women	1980	1990	Men 1990
Botswana	0.8%	2.8%	3.4%
Iraq	5.6%	9.8%	15.4%
Sri Lanka	2.4%	4.1%	6.2%
Turkey	2.9%	9.1%	16.4%
Morocco	2.7%	7.3%	12.3%

This is complemented by low enrolment by women students in scientific disciplines, particularly in Africa:

1990	Natural Sciences	Medicine
Benin	10%	17%
Nigeria	19%	25%
Uganda	12%	22%
Bangladesh	15%	27%
El Salvador	15%	20%

(*Source: World Education Report* 1993)

Statistical analysis needs to be viewed with extreme caution as there are a number of extenuating factors. For example, women frequently outnumber men in the student body but this figure can result from a change in the definition of higher education and the emergence of degrees in fields such as Nursing or Teaching. Similarly, women are still far too few in high technology courses and thus cannot expect the resulting career returns. On this point, more numerous initiatives such as that taken by the American National Science Foundation offering sponsored courses to encourage women's enrolment are required. And yet, many industrialized countries are in fact failing to fill all available places in scientific courses. A recent OECD report noted that the demand for engineers exceeded the available supply of graduates in 10 West European countries. (*From Higher Education to Employment*, OECD 1993). Hence, the specifically female dimension of a problem must always be studied in a wider context.

Notwithstanding these factors, certain aspects of the access/ participation analysis require significant improvement, notably a) further analysis of the courses chosen by women, b) the fortunes of female graduates when they become predominant in a given profession yet fail to share in the decision-making process of that field, and c) the promotion of women in science at all levels of education so as to permit careers in this domain.

From the economic standpoint, higher education qualifications effectively raise both employment prospects and social expectations of graduates. Despite the current economic climate, those with a degree or diploma are ten times more likely to find employment that unskilled persons. Thus, it is high time to promote more enlightened attitudes towards highly educated women whose qualifications entitle them to career fulfilment and who - as the principal or equal salary-earner - require appropriate support in the management of personal and professional duties.

In this climate, the question must be raised as to whether women will be permitted to claim their right to participation in higher education decision-making. A major research study underway is investigating whether women in the academy have the necessary confidence and will to assert their contribution to knowledge and policy development (Bond, 1994-1996), and its first results are included in this book. There is still a doubt that support is symbolic. Only massive affirmative action can swell the numbers to the proportions needed or give formal recognition of the existing critical mass so as to bring about the required difference. Moreover, attitudinal change is perhaps the most critical factor to effect significant improvement. As the quality and relevance of higher education depend ultimately on the excellence of its personnel, the moment is indeed propitious for sweeping away the barriers which still exist. If such an experiment meets with success in higher education, then progress in other professional fields may be facilitated as well.

Trends towards Change

The world is moving towards greater democracy and market-oriented policies in an effort to improve human development. In this climate, more opportunities should be provided for women to obtain executive appointments. The efforts of women's groups and the resolutions of international conferences all contribute towards the recruitment of women for such positions.

Clear trends to strengthen the empowerment of highly qualified women are visible in the fields of research, training, advocacy and networking. These operate both in the higher education domain itself and also in professional activities. UNESCO, as the UN agency for Education, concentrates its efforts in the higher education sub-sector. However, the spin-off effects resulting from increased access and participation are life-long and have flow-on benefits for women in all social groups.

Research is essential in order to provide an accurate knowledge base for affirmative action. This is well-advanced in the industrialized world, but still too rare in developing countries. One good example, however, is the research carried out by the African Academy of Sciences on women's access to education in this region. Furthermore, Women's Studies, as a university discipline, is fast becoming a focal point for the monitoring and analysis of women's social and economic empowerment. Once dismissed as an esoteric domain, it can now provide the data needed to support the call for change. A successful case was the institutionalization of the Gender Studies course at the University of the West Indies which constituted a base for further research and training action in favour of women - both on campus and in Caribbean society.

Solid research results justify and facilitate the provision of **training**. This may be aimed at empowering women for decision-making roles in all fields; or it may aim at strengthening the management skills of women academics and administrators in particular - an example being the Higher Education Resource Services (HERS) seminars, run by the Office for Higher Education of the American Council for Education. In this latter area, UNESCO has set up UNITWIN networks with the Association of Commonwealth Universities for Africa and Asia, and with the Inter-American Organization for Higher Education (IOHE) for the Latin American region. These activities are already yielding positive results.

Advocacy can be more eloquent if based on solid and accurate information. Permanent monitoring groups are needed to fulfil this role and to sensitize policy makers. This task is often effectively undertaken by regional bodies such as the Forum for African Women Educationalists (FAWE), by ministries, by Equal Employment Officers in higher education institutions as well as by IGOs and NGOs.

Networking is a strategy which underpins advocacy because it strengthens and increases the actual number of voices in favour of women's empowerment. In order to promote the advancement of women in society there is a need for approaches which require research, training and exchange programmes. Many organizations for this purpose have been set up in Africa, Asia, Latin America and the Caribbean and higher education institutions are closely involved. Non-governmental organizations take part in such programmes as do regional bodies. For instance, the Employment Experts Network of the European Parliament tracks the presence and status of women in professional fields, while the European Network for Women's Studies, launched by UNESCO's European Centre for Higher Education (CEPES) with the Council of Europe, links some 1,700 researchers in 24 countries. UNESCO assists both regional and international training programmes for university women. More of this action is required in the developing world where highly qualified women are frequently in a strong position to advocate positive change.

V. Women and the University Curriculum

Guiding Principles
The inclusion of gender issues in the university curriculum can be justified on several counts:

- **recognition and enhancement of the university's role in society.** In this respect, the UNESCO Policy Paper on Higher Education makes a plea for social equity as well as for managerial efficiency. Indeed, the latter cannot be an end in itself but rather, should facilitate the social effectiveness of higher education institutions and their graduates. Hence, access becomes a right which should be observed since the overall benefits of well-educated and trained citizens - male and female - are great for all countries;
- **impact of the Internationalization (or Globalization) phenomenon.** This impact is so great that no sphere can avoid its implications. Thus, the university curriculum must be reviewed and modernized in all spheres to take account of the challenges of global change -a process which is affecting women in many ways;
- **the creation and exchange of knowledge and know-how**. Following from the previous point, the aim is now to generate expertise which is internationally accredited but locally applicable. Since this underpins the development process both globally and in each region, it has major ramifications for all groups in society including women;
- **the need to tackle social problems at the grass-roots level**. As women play a major role in development, concrete strategies must be found to increase awareness of this. Within the higher education sector, renovation of the university curriculum is one useful way to sensitize a wider public to gender issues and to ensure the actuality and relevance of the knowledge gained;
- **mainstreaming of gender issues.** The foregoing efforts are designed to achieve this ultimate goal which is only correct and equitable since women represent 50% of humanity. At the

same time, mainstreaming accords correct status to gender questions.

From Policy to Co-operative Action

The UNESCO Policy Paper sets down the key principles for renewal in higher education policy-making. From this basis, UNESCO collaborates with its numerous partners - Member States, IGOs and NGOs and the intellectual community - in order to translate policy issues into practical action.

The main instrument for this process is the UNITWIN/UNESCO Chairs Programme which was launched in 1991 and has helped create some 200 Chairs and inter-university networks across all regions. All these projects aim at promoting sustainable development via the generation and sharing of high-level expertise. The programme reflects the growing awareness of the crucial role of higher education in the modern world in which socio-economic development is increasingly knowledge-intensive and is relying more heavily than before on highly-skilled human resources. From this perspective, university teaching, training and research obviously assume new significance.

Perhaps the really innovative aspect of the UNITWIN/UNESCO Chairs Programme is found in the fields of study selected by the participating institutions. Demography, the Environment, Community Health, Literacy, the Global Economy, Women and Development, the Transfer of Technology, Human Rights and Peace Studies - these are some of the domains where complex issues arise and necessitate a multi-disciplinary approach in order to propose ground-breaking solutions.

The Programme places special emphasis not only on the North/South axis of co-operation but also on the South/South dimension. Here, the intention is to alleviate the Brain Drain which is the negative result of the mobility phenomenon and which has provoked disastrous results for the developing world.

A principal partner in the UNITWIN/UNESCO Chairs Programme is the United Nations University. Based on Tokyo, its mission is to promote multi-disciplinary research and training on global problems. In his address to the 4th Collective Consultation on Higher Education (Paris, September 1994), the acting Academic Vice-Rector of the UNU stressed the need to understand the major trends re-shaping the world order and the powerful forces of change driving contemporary history. These are causing large-scale social transformation at an ever-accelerated pace. Hence, the UNU agenda covers 5 thematic clusters: peace and human security, economic change, population welfare, science and technology and environmental phenomena.

In effect, the United Nations University - whose research results are available to all UNITWIN and UNESCO Chair projects - constitutes a bridge between traditional academia and international co-operation. The former is concerned with the generation and transmission of knowledge; the latter - led by the UN system - promotes dialogue between the family of nations for the good of their common future.

Both the UNITWIN/UNESCO Chairs Programme and the UNU recognize that the gender dimension of these issues is a factor which is crucial to their analysis and resolution. For this reason, Women and Development has emerged as a vital domain where training and research must be intensified.

Building on the NGO inter-university networks already operating to promote leadership training and management skills for women academics and administrators, a new project for ten UNESCO Chairs will be launched in 1996 on the theme of **Women, Higher Education and Human Development.** These will address special problems of women in selected fields inter alia, rural development and community health, population education, the role of water resources in socio-economic development, the evolution and impact of women's studies and the rights of women migrants and refugees. Support from the established management and leadership networks will be beneficial as these provide a framework which affirms the rights of women and responsibilities of women as professionals and as citizens in society.

The relevance of these selected fields for traditional disciplines is clear. However, the problems involved require a new perspective and multi-disciplinary curriculum design - hence greater inter-faculty collaboration will be desirable.

VI. The Beijing Declaration and Platform for Action: Implications for the University Curriculum

This document, adopted by the 4th World Conference on Women, merits special mention because it provides the latest link between women and current global development concerns.

Its Mission Statement eloquently expresses its purpose and long-term intentions:

"The Platform of Action is an agenda for women's empowerment. It aims at accelerating the implementation of the Nairobi Forward-looking strategies for the Advancement of Women and removing all the obstacles to women's active participation in all spheres of public and private life through a full and equal share in economic, social, cultural and political decision-making. This means that the principle of shared power and responsibility should be established between women and men at home, in the workplace and in the wider national and international communities. Equality between men and women is a matter of human rights and a condition for social justice and is also a necessary and fundamental pre-requisite for equality, development and peace. A transformed partnership based on equality between women and men is a condition for people-centred sustainable development. A sustained and long-term commitment is essential so that women and men can work together for themselves, for their children and for society to meet the challenges of the twenty-first century." (Chapter 1)

Furthermore, this document calls upon governments, NGOs and the private sector to be active partners in implementing its objectives. During the preparations for Beijing, the text was debated in regional fora which have sought to relate its priorities to their own particular agendas for development. Both regionally and internationally, the academic community has a major role to play in this call to action.

The Beijing Declaration and Platform for Action has relevance for the following collection of case studies because it clearly defines those critical concerns affecting women and their development:

- the persistent burden of poverty;
- inequality of access to education, health and welfare;
- violence;
- the effects of armed conflicts;
- absence from decision-making in economic structures and policies and in the productive process;
- inequality in the sharing of power and decision-making at all levels of society;
- insufficient mechanisms to promote the advancement of women;
- inadequate awareness of and commitment to women's human rights;
- the inadequate portrayal of women's contribution to society by the mass media;
- insufficient recognition and support for their contribution to the management of natural resources and the environment.

These issues are directly linked to academic disciplines, notably Economics, Public Policy and Administration, Education, Health, Law, the Sciences, Technology and Communication. In addition, the opportunities for multi-disciplinary analysis offered by emerging fields such as Development, Environmental and Peace

Studies are rich in potential. Last but certainly not least, the broad and over-arching knowledge gained though Literature, Philosophy and cross-cultural studies enhances understanding of humanity and thus of the specific questions affecting women.

The authors of these studies - all experts in diverse fields and representing the international academic community - were invited to be critical by identifying inadequate curricula and by describing good practice so that sensitization can develop into supportive action and positive attitudinal shift. In this way, they are suggesting innovative responses for educators in a variety of disciplines who are facing the challenges of teaching and learning in a rapidly changing and uncertain world. As a result of such an approach, according to the conclusions reached by Malcolm Skilbeck in *Curriculum Reform: an Overview of Trends*,

"... students are encouraged to develop skills of analysis and communication, to be problem-solvers, flexible thinkers, adaptable people." (1990: 75)

These studies show that it has become vital - and indeed urgent - to know whether and how gender issues are addressed in various disciplines. And, if this is not the case, universities need to know how this can be best achieved since they do not wish to retain outdated curricula. Furthermore, they demonstrate the discrepancies which exist and the progress to be made. This range of experiences also attests to the common goal increasingly shared by women graduates worldwide -namely, that their contribution to society must be better understood and their rights and responsibilities must be fully acknowledged. In this manner, their true potential can be realized.

Indeed, a strategy for change can be elaborated based on four key premises.

- **The promotion of feminine leadership in the academy**

Sheryl Bond examines the concept of academic leadership today, emphasizing that the increasing appointment of women indicates the reality of social change. Factors preventing women's access to top positions are considered and new paradigms witnessing the interaction of social context and positional power are described. Bond advocates a move from debate to dialogue which will equate the advancement of women with the renewal of the institution - an essential shift in thinking if higher education is to contribute effectively to the development process.

- **The mainstreaming of the gender dimension in the curriculum**

Without exception, the authors believe that this must guide curriculum development in the future. Writing on gender and the law in the African context, Henrietta Mensa-Bonsu stresses that universities are a vital source of women's empowerment through their teaching and research functions. Mainstreaming legal issues as they pertain to women is a means of ensuring that these questions will be taken seriously.

This view is echoed by Maria Inacia d'Avila Neto, a Brazilian expert on interdisciplinarity related to development. She insists on the dangers resulting from separate or marginalized gender studies since the progress of women must be studied in relation to overall social and economic change - for this reason, gender sensitivity becomes a crucial element in the educational process.

Further support for mainstreaming is expressed in the field of Medicine. Sandra Levison and Katherine Sherif discuss the importance of training doctors in attitudes to health and gender where significant socio-economic and cultural factors come into play. Awareness of these is the foundation of a woman-centred health curriculum in medical training.

In Commerce and Business, Margaret Gardner (Australia) notes the predominant male character of these fields which must now evolve as women's enrolment continues to grow, thereby creating a critical mass amongst student numbers. The principle of gender inclusion is evoked as a strategy to ensure equity in these disciplines and to encourage women to pursue their chosen professional studies with confidence.

- **Continued research on barriers to women's equality**

Authors strongly agreed that analysis of such obstacles must not be abandoned since this can provide reliable evidence of women's progress towards equal status in society. For example, Anne Holden Rønning (Norway) comments that Literature, Languages and History offer extremely varied perspectives on women, illustrating that gender is not an issue invented in the twentieth century. She regrets that research is too often neglected in the Humanities despite its proven contribution to the monitoring of social change and the impact of this on women's lives.

In an analysis of the best approach to teaching the new field of Women's Studies in Bulgaria, Ralitsa Muharska considers that the country's current state of social transition is, itself, a major barrier to feminine equality. Gender cannot be simply an academic discipline. It must relate to social reality and lead to the empowerment of women - otherwise it will have little attraction or credibility for students. It is also noted that, as is the case elsewhere, Women's Studies do not offer wide career prospects beyond the academic context.

Two perennially problematic areas - Science and Technology and Teacher Training - are treated in case studies from the People's Republic of China, New Zealand and Israel. For the former, Gui Zhizhen and Robyn Dormer consider the well-known barriers preventing women from excelling in scientific disciplines, notably the absence of sufficient role models, a lack of encouragement and confidence-building for gifted girls and the limited attractiveness of scientific careers in a world where service industries beckon. These obstacles are strong deterrents when coupled with the struggle faced by women attempting to balance family responsibilities with the stringent demands of a career in scientific research. Nevertheless, a call is made to teach these fields differently, placing emphasis on their social applications. These are very real and help facilitate "...wider ranging understandings of gender and science in society." (McGregor and Harding: 4)

Rina Shachar, a specialist in teacher education, is critical of the wasted potential resulting from gender inequality which is perpetuated by incorrect attitudes instilled in children from their early childhood. Stereotyping, the persistence of low expectations for talented girls and discouraging parental attitudes compound to prevent women from reaching optimal personal or professional achievement. Her Intervention Model of Gender Equality, to be used in teacher training courses, promotes awareness, understanding and the capacity to effect change amongst children and their parents. This concluding chapter is a reminder that, since higher education is closely linked to other levels of the system, the gender dimension cannot be omitted at any stage.

- **The Gender Dimension of Development**

According to the majority of authors, acknowledgement of this reality has emerged in recent years as a key innovation to be included in the future university curriculum. This view corroborates the conclusions of the 1995 Human Development Report which states that development problems will remain unresolved until the status of women is raised,

Convincing evidence is provided by Maria Teresa Gallego and Otilia Mó who have studied training for the civil service in Spain. In a country where enormous social and economic evolution has occurred in the last two decades, these authors contend that public policy-making must be modernized in its vision and management so as to ensure the quality of the change process - where women play a dominant role as citizens and in the work force.

It would be useful to review the academic curriculum related to Public Administration in order to take into account the priorities of social progress such as enhanced services in the education, health and local government sectors.

According to Mouna Samman, awareness of the gender dimension is now a desirable aspect of the Demography curriculum. In the past, this discipline was taught in a neutral manner with a strong focus on statistical data. However, the cultural specificities of the field can no longer be ignored in view of its relation to the development process. Women now have a better understanding of numerous factors which profoundly shape their lives - for instance, the link between fertility control and empowerment and the consequences of dependence in patriarchal societies. It is thus important that their choices be informed and the role of education is a main instrument in this regard.

A youth perspective on gender and development is provided by Willemijn Tuinstra, an Agronomy student at Wageningen Agricultural University in the Netherlands. In the developing world, women play a central role in the production and management of food resources - and hence to nutrition, community health and poverty reduction. In the industrialized countries, women are entering this profession in increasing numbers. Yet, their contribution has yet to be fully recognized. An organization such as the International Association of Agricultural Students (IAAS) can have significant impact in several ways - by sensitizing members to the gender aspect and by encouraging field studies which facilitate their understanding of this. One direct result is that students demand curricular changes to reflect more adequately the reality of their chosen field. Moreover, this chapter illustrates international dialogue amongst young people from different cultures allows them to appreciate more profoundly the complexity of global issues.

Last but not least, the gender dimension is very real in national or regional contexts where aggression prevails. Sanáa Osseiran is a researcher in peace studies, which have democracy and equality as their prime objectives. She evokes the many situations in which women face conflict - in law and human rights, in employment and in social exclusion. Moreover, she proposes that women who have helped foster peace through their personal and professional lives should be promoted as role models for conflict-resolution. Several university disciplines ranging from Law and Economics to Sociology and Women's Studies could accommodate this strategy.

VII. Conclusions: Beyond Beijing

The issues discussed in this chapter are intended to show that higher education and the development process which aims at equality, democracy and peace are closely connected. Consequently, the particular interests of women in both these areas must be given full consideration. For these reasons, the university curriculum has become a vital tool for achieving significant improvement in resolving the many problems related to women in today's world.

It should be reiterated that higher education equips women both for professional activity and for society itself.

In professional life, the complexity of the obstacles to women's promotion to decision-making levels suggests that substantial change will not be realized through an evolutionary process. The short-term measure is for international, government and business and commercial sectors to take affirmative action to significantly increase the proportion of women at the decision-making level. Target setting, a progressive move towards equality and closer monitoring of women's appointments to decision-making levels in the various economic and social sectors remain priorities even if resistance can be expected.

To this end, UNESCO's recent Social Science research has heightened awareness of women's contribution to the processes of social and economic development. Studies such as "Women and the Informal Sector (1992) and "Women in Developing Economies" (1993) have shed light on the magnitude of this contribution and, regrettably, on its lack of adequate recognition. Similarly, further research has focused on women in fields such as public policy making (1990), the media (1987) and their role in transitional economies (1991), thus demonstrating that the reality of their presence fully justifies their involvement in decision-making.

At the same time, the special contribution made by highly qualified women to social development - which implies progress towards higher living standards, greater equality of opportunity and basic human rights for all peoples and nations - must be constantly emphasized. Clearly, equality, development and peace can never be realized while grave social and economic imbalances pertain. A country's social and economic progress as well as its ability to adapt to a changing environment depend largely on the quality of its human resources whose education and training must be sound yet flexible and thus able to adapt to changing conditions. Higher Education graduates have a special task in this endeavour. Through the ethical conduct of their family, community and professional lives, they play a key role in guiding society towards a state of more equitable development which greatly enhances the quality of life for the under-privileged members of society.

In the light of the present world climate, all men and women have an equal responsibility to use their empowerment for the purposes of equality, democracy and peace. These principles guided the debate at the 4th World Conference on Women but efforts must extend beyond Beijing to bring about genuine progress towards attaining these goals. Higher education and the academic community have their specific role in this endeavour. In conclusion therefore, what is learnt in universities - and how this is used - is of the greatest importance both for women themselves and for humanity in general.

Bibliography

An Agenda for Development. United Nations, New York, 1995.

An Agenda for Peace. United Nations, New York, 1995.

Bould, David and Grahame Feletti. *The Challenge of Problem-based Learning.* Kogan Page, London, 1991.

Education: a Means for Empowering Girls and Women. UNESCO, Paris, 1994.

Harding, Sandra and Elizabeth McGregor. *The Gender Dimension of Science and*
Technology. UNESCO, Paris, 1995.

Higher Education and Capacity-building for the 21st Century. Report of the 4th UNESCO/NGO Collective Consultation on Higher Education. UNESCO, Paris, 1995.

Higher Education: The Lessons of Experience. World Bank, 1994.

Higher Education Staff Development: Directions for the 21st Century. UNESCO, Paris, 1994, 170 p.

Human Development Report 1993. UNDP, 1993.

Husén, Torsten (Ed.). *The Role of the University - A Global Perspective.* UNESCO, Paris; UNU, Tokyo, 1994, 231 p.

Improving Women's Access to Higher Education. Dundar and Haworth, World Bank, 1993.

King, Elizabeth M. and Hill, Anne M. (Eds.) *Women's Education in Developing Countries.* World Bank, 1993.

Policy Paper for Change and Development in Higher Education. UNESCO, Paris, 1995, 43 p.

Reports of the UNESCO/NGO Collective Consultations. UNESCO 1988, 1991, 1992.

La Responsabilité des femmes dans la conduite de leur carrière et enseignement supérieur. Rapport de la Table Ronde UNESCO/FIFDU, 1988.
Skilbeck, Malcolm. *Curriculum Reform. An Overview of Trends.* OECD, Paris, 1990.

Social Development, Women and Higher Education. UNESCO/IFUW Submission to the Commission on Education for the XXI Century, UNESCO, 1994.

The Beijing Declaration and Platform for Action. Document adopted by the 4th World Conference on Women, United Nations, 1995.

The Human Development Report. UNDP 1993, 1994, 1995.

The Jobs Study: Facts, Analysis, Strategies. OECD, 1994.

Women in Higher Education Management. UNESCO/Commonwealth Secretariat, 1993.

The World Education Report. UNESCO, Paris, 1993, 1994

The World Science Report. UNESCO, Paris, 1994.

World Social Summit 1995: UNESCO Position Paper. UNESCO, 1994.

The Experience of Feminine Leadership in the Academy

Sheryl L. Bond
Queen's University, Ontario, Canada

Introduction

The fundamental changes which are occurring worldwide in the areas of democratization, globalization, regionalization, polarization, marginalization and technology, are transforming societies. This transformation, while important and necessary, is often painfully difficult for people and the institutions which provide the social and political framework for inter-personal and international relationships.

To steer societies through the course of events and to emerge from the transformation closer to achieving peace, democracy, and sustainable development, is a formidable challenge requiring all the available talent, experience, and expertise in society and must include the effective utilization of the talent, experience and expertise of women at all levels of decision-making.

The principle and practice of full and equal partnership of women and men is in itself a significant transformation in gender roles, and is yet to be achieved. To the extent that the partnership is underdeveloped, so too is the ability of society to address the other critical areas of transformation. This transformation in gender roles is a process which in itself can and is being altered by increased public awareness, research, dialogue and an array of interventions.

Education, as it is manifested in its various types and levels of institutions, has a special formative and exemplary role to play in the development of society. Those holding leadership posts in educational institutions in general, and in higher education institutions in particular, play an uniquely important role in shaping the institution which plays such a crucial role in shaping society and the future.

It is critical, therefore, that there be an equal partnership of women and men in mid to senior decision-making posts within the academy in order that women provide an intellectual and moral leadership which will embrace the experience of women.

Leadership in the Academy

Leadership can and does occur in the domains of teaching, research, and administration. Teachers define who will be taught, what will be taught, how it will be taught and the standards of evaluating what has been learned. Leaders in teaching are imbued with an extraordinary ability to know what knowledge is most critical to teach, excite students and peers about learning, know what teaching practices are most effective, and invest their considerable energies in the promotion of student learning.

Researchers define questions and seek answers. Leaders in research have the ability to identify and answer particularly important questions, seek connectivity and are driven to communicate their work to others.

Administrative leadership is the force which guides the university. Administrative positions at the senior level are vested with the responsibility, whether derived by statute, charter, or articles of incorporation, for ensuring that the institution and its members fulfill their educational, social, and ethical mandates. In a university, leadership responsibilities reside both in the position and with the individual who holds the office at any point in time. Administrative leaders may or may not be leaders in either teaching or research but, are respected for their judgment, institutional knowledge, and predictive powers. Such individuals are usually drawn into the institutional structure through appointment to senior administrative posts.

While holding a leadership position does not in itself guarantee a person is a leader, the administrative leader speaks to the academy, including its students, staff and external constituencies, about what the academy is, what it is doing or could be doing better, and provides a contextual framework with which to guide the institution's progress towards its goals. In so doing, the senior administrator, through the use of influence, shapes the standards and, through the judicious use of authority, monitors the application of those standards to the appointment of those admitted to the professoriate, and as well as those identified as leaders.

Appointing Women Leaders

Institutional filters

To a large extent, the adaptive capacity of an institution is determined by the ability of that institution to identify leaders and draw them into senior administrative posts. Who is seen to be a leader and selected, either through nomination, selection or appointment to take up senior administrative posts, is critical to the quality of the institution. There is ample evidence that there exist "filters", unrelated to ability, through which leaders must pass in order to be posted to administrative positions of significant influence.

Selection criteria based upon preferred personal style, class status and gender are examples of filters which diminish the available pool of leaders considered desirable for appointment to senior administrative posts. This filtering process may be explicit or implicit but, either way, it marginalizes an important portion of the talent and expertise needed to address urgent human issues and in doing so the university diminishes its own ability to seek truth and conduct its work in a meaningful and effective manner.

There is strong evidence of a tendency for those making the selection to pick persons who are non-threatening, or most like themselves. In general, those making the selection of individuals for appointments to senior decision-making positions are men.

Personal filters
In addition to the continuing presence of inappropriate institutional filters, we have gathered data which indicates that (a) some women, like some men, accept senior administrative posts if offered but, (b) unlike most men, some women, who possess the attributes and experience which is sought by institutions, are deciding to shape their career in such a way as to preclude their appointment to senior leadership posts. While focusing one's life's work in the other domains of academic life may also bring about significant contributions to research and teaching, the moderately small numbers of women currently in the "pool" for senior administrative appointment are, nonetheless, diminished. While protecting the right of a woman to choose a career path which does not include the responsibilities of administrative leadership, it is important to ensure that this choice is not an outcome of policies or practices of the institution which tell a woman she is not valued in a leadership capacity and/or that her realities (other commitments) will not be taken into account when structuring the terms of such an appointment.

Whether through the operation of blatant discriminatory practices, the more subtle but inappropriate institutional filters in the appointment process, or a woman's personal choice of career, the fact remains that while women make up over 50% of the students in some disciplines and 17% of the professoriate, fewer than 10% of those appointed to senior administrative posts are women. Such simple numerical data make it apparent that the domain of leadership at the senior decision-making levels in universities remains the domain of men.

An unequal partnership

If the moral imperative to bring women into senior administrative positions is strong and the adaptability as well as the quality of the institution are at stake, why are there still so few women?

A comprehensive programme of action research, has over the last three years, been examining this question from the personal perspective of women and men in Canadian universities, who currently hold senior administrative positions, or who would be considered in the "pool" of candidates for appointment to senior positions in institutions of higher education.

Data gathered from smaller, pilot studies alerted us to the strong possibility that the social context within which women and the institution function might well be an important factor in understanding how decision-making, within a strong academic ethos, differs within different contemporary contexts. Parallel studies in Latin America, India and English-speaking Africa have been launched and the data available from Spanish-speaking Latin America will be discussed.

The Canadian context

The use of an extensive comparator set of Canadian data provides an opportunity to account for two important variables, (a) legal protection against discrimination, and (b) availability of suitable candidates for appointment.

There exists in Canadian legislation, at both the national and provincial level, actively enforced institutional policies, to prevent discrimination against women in hiring and promotion, and in some cases, to begin to redress historic imbalances. The legislation has force through compliance requirements for institutional funding and through the existence of accessible enforcement tribunals.

Secondly, moderate numbers of women suitably qualified for appointment to leadership positions in academia do now exist in Canada. Significant progress in appointing women to decision-making posts, particularly at the departmental and decanal levels within the university, has been achieved. Nonetheless, such progress is highly inconsistent among institutions, and overall it is not as great as might be expected from the availability of suitable appointees in a context free from official discrimination.

These results point to (a) the existence of additional barriers and (b) a tempering of results which can be expected from the removal of these barriers to the appointment of significant numbers of women to senior decision making posts. Identifying the determinants of behaviour which facilitate or block the appointment of women is a more complex problem than earlier studies had postulated. New studies, using methodological approaches which provide for a wider range of variables, are required.

Using a new paradigm to examine complex behaviour

The continuing underutilization of the talent and expertise of women within the university has been identified not only as an unacceptable form of discrimination but as a significant deterrent to the quality and the adaptability of the institution and society. The fact of the continuing dearth of women in senior administrative positions in organizations, in general, has been the subject of investigation, discussion and, frequently, divisive debate. In this regard, two theoretical perspectives have dominated.

The first perspective is a person-centered view in which the paucity of women is attributed to the psycho-social attributes, including personality characteristics, attitudes and behavioral skills of women themselves. The "problem" is vested in the individual and she is called upon to adapt herself to the traditional, male concept of management within the academy.

An alternate theoretical perspective emerged to explain the data. The structure-centered paradigm advances the view that it is the disadvantageous position of women in the organizational structures (few numbers, little power, limited access to resources) which shapes and defines the behavior of women. The underlying premise of this perspective is that men and women are equally capable and committed to assuming positions of leadership . The "problem" is vested in the structure, and the remedy is a fundamental change to eliminate inappropriate discrimination in institutional policies and practices.

Despite the initial optimism of their respective creators, neither perspective has been able to explain the continuing lack of significant progress of women. In addition, the "exclusivity" inherent in each paradigm may well have generated more divisiveness than dialogue as answers and remedies continue to be sought. Neither paradigm made provision for the possibility of an interactive effect between the two variables, nor did either anticipate the possibility that the power of the position might, in itself, be an important determinant of a person's behavior. Flaws in the assumptions and the methodology of gathering and analyzing data appear to have led to overly simplistic interpretations of the findings.

In the attempt to address the methodological problems identified in earlier studies, we used a paradigm in which both simple comparisons and multivariate analysis of variance could be run to account for the effect of **gender** (sex/personal attributes), **positional power** (level of administrative appointment, access to resources, value of the person's knowledge and expertise to the institution) and **societal context** (Canada and Latin America). Other special features of the studies make them different from earlier studies.

Special features of the current studies

These studies have certain special features.

- We studied the population of women within academe who already hold vice-presidencies, directorships, deanships and department headships and by virtue of their experience and expertise are the "pool" from which appointments to senior decision making positions will be drawn. These are talented, highly educated and experienced women who have differentiated their lives from those of other women. In the first instance, they made the decision to pursue their intellectual interests within the framework of a university. Secondly, by virtue of having gained access to positions of administrative leadership within the institution, they have differentiated themselves from their academic peers .

- These large-scale studies included the entire population of university administrators in Canada and a stratified random sample of university administrators in Spanish-speaking Latin America.

- The working hypotheses is that a person is both changed by the position the person holds and the social context within which the person works and, at the same time, changes them.

- The framing of the questions as well as the gathering and analysis of the data took into account the potential interaction between gender, positional power, and societal context.

Although women make up less than 10 percent of the administrative population studied, over 42% of those participating in the study are women.

The personal experience of administrative leadership

Using a combination of qualitative and quantitative measures and the methodological approach described above, 3500 people, in the parallel Canadian and Latin American studies, reported on their perceptions and experiences as university administrators. This perspective from the field had, in earlier pilot studies, provided the useful vantage point from which to view the disjunctures between policy and practice between the individual experience and the broader social realities.

In the very early stages of the research, administrators identified a range of personal, positional, and institutional attributes as being particularly influential in the formulation of their perceptions of themselves as leaders and in their expectations of being appointed to senior decision-making posts. Among the 12 subscales and over 140 measures identified and examined, those measures reported on here include (1) the importance of work, (2) the integration of work and home (3) life priorities and commitments, (4) attributions for appointment, (5) career aspiration and expectation for advancement, (6) obstacles to being offered or accepting a more senior administrative post, and (7) the impact of the professional (institutional) climate on self-esteem and effectiveness.

Highlights of the Findings to Date

The data from the Canadian and Latin American studies continue to be analyzed and follow-up has begun with small focus groups to discuss the findings. Highlights of the findings to date include:

1. The Need for Peer Interaction

Institutional autonomy, which is a university tradition, militates against the creation of any centralized data base about persons in leadership positions. The absence of such information makes it difficult to investigate a whole range of phenomena about higher education and, consequently, makes it more likely that policy will be set based on conjecture rather than fact.

Not knowing who holds administrative posts within the university system also undermines the ability of women to interact and consult with their peers. Because numbers are moderately low, women have a greater need for inter-institutional inter-disciplinary networking which is not normally available.

2. Lack of Role Differentiation

We found a high degree of gender ambiguity (i.e. lack of role differentiation) in both the Canadian and Latin American studies. Initially, we defined "gender" as a set of prescribed roles attributed to women and men which are understood to be inculcated very early through the family and later through education and employment. A well tested personal attribute scale was included in the studies as a way to examine role attributes, over time, with gender.

Both the Canadian and Latin American data, however, indicated such a significant degree of role "ambiguity" (as opposed to role differentiation) between men and women that a perusal of all but one of the 24 personal attribute measures would not permit identification of the respondent's gender with even a modest probability of success.

Although we reported the personal attributions which did differentiate the behaviour of females from males, the term gender for the purpose of these studies, could only be defined as sex (male/female) and not personal attributes.

3. Diversity amongst Women

The data on personal attributes indicates that significant diversity exists amongst women. This finding challenges the position often taken in the public and sometimes political debates that women, as a group, think and act differently from men as a group. This reported diversity appears in spite of similarity of age, educational attainment and family status. To a limited extent, however, this diversity in personal attributes is moderated by the level of positional power held by the respondent.

4. Characteristics of Female Administrators
Although there is considerable role ambiguity, characteristics of female administrators are differentiated from their male counterparts. These are evident in three areas.

Background
Similar to the findings of considerable role ambiguity on the personal attribute scale, women and men reported having more similar than different educational training and work experiences preparing them for their academic career. The only difference in the experiential or technical background that was found. Women reported taking many more continuing professional education courses, especially in the area of management, than did men.

Age and Stage
Women in the studies are slightly younger than their male peers at all administrative levels, and they are more likely to currently hold administrative appointments at the departmental or decanal levels and in inter-disciplinary institutes or research centers than in the higher levels of administrative posts in the institution.

Attributes of Leadership
Women and men described themselves as being moderately dominant (as opposed to passive) in interactions, more gentle than tough on people, more helpful to others, competitive, self confident, and able to stand up well under pressure. The ability to stay calm in a crisis and stand up well under pressure increased with the seniority of the administrative appointment.

Perceptions and Experiences
Even with these large numbers of respondents of both sexes, the perceptions and experiences of women and men, although often not exactly the same, did not differ significantly on most measures. Using a 1% confidence interval on all simple comparisons and 5% on all multivariate analysis of variance,

25% of the 120 measures studied found significant gender differences were initially identified on 25% of the 120 measures. A re-examination of these findings using a multivariate analysis of variance for gender and level of administrative position found nearly half of these differences reported were caused either by positional power or the societal context within which the respondents worked.

Positional Power

Many of the findings of significance could be accounted for by the level of the administrative position held by the respondent, and not gender. This was especially the case for the measures on the professional climate subscale. Better known as the "chilly climate", we replicated the familiar and well documented indicators from earlier studies which have examined this phenomenon. Controlling for level of administrative post of the respondent, we found no significant gender differences in the 15 indicators studied. Earlier studies which found significant gender differences and which did not control for level of position may have made a mistaken attribution of the cause of the differences.

Marginalization of talented people

An institutional culture and its decision-making structure which covets talent in the domains of teaching and research but not in its administrative leaders, regardless of whether that leadership is exercised by a woman or a man, may pose a significant problem to the overall quality of the institution.

Gender and Societal Context

The interaction between gender and societal context (G x S) produced significant differences in the Canadian and Latin American data on measures of :

Marital status: thirty-six percent of the women and eleven per cent of the men in the Latin American study reported they were married. The situation was just the reverse in Canada where 76% of the men and 33 percent of the women reported married.

Personal attributes: women in the Latin American study reported having more difficulty with decision-making, and getting their feelings hurt more easily than did women in the Canadian study. While Canadian women reported being much more independent than did their Latin American peers, they also expressed a much stronger need for security. Although reporting to be more dependent, Latin American women reported very low level needs for security as well as much stronger ties to family.

Gender Differences

Significant gender differences (G), which could not be accounted for by a multivariate analysis of variance with level of position or societal context, were found for the following measures:

Personal attributes
Women in both studies reported that more often than not they cried easily, were emotional, needful of others approval, aware of others feelings and warm in relations with others.

Divergence in attributes
While the responses of men on most measures of personal attributes tended to move in the same direction on the scale as did the responses of women, there were two measures on which the responses of women and men were divergent. First, men, in both studies, reported being much more home than career oriented and women reported being much more career oriented than home oriented. Second, men reported they rarely cried at all and women reported crying easily. While the latter attribute has been examined in many studies, the divergence on the career/home orientation with the men reporting a strong home orientation has not previously been reported and requires further examination.

Importance of work
Women in both studies rank their current administrative responsibilities as being the most important thing in their total life. Men ranked their current work as somewhat less than the most important.

Factors attributed as being influential to administrative appointments
Women in both studies reported they achieved their current administrative appointment through their own efforts (they sought out and worked to get it). In addition, women attributed their success to the encouragement of family, friends and peers, their ideas and vision and the continuing professional education courses which they had taken.

Men attributed their appointment to being nominated, and to their years of experience and their work as an academic. It may be that men, expecting senior appointments to naturally come their way, felt they would wait until they were sought out or alternately, the traditional cultural ethos in the academy that one should not admit to aspirations for leadership may be more strongly felt by the men than the women. The fact that women do aspire and seek senior decision-making responsibilities may in itself be problematic to their appointment to such positions. Selection committees remain the domain of men and men have reported being wary of such behaviour.

Obstacles to appointment
Although both women and men indicated that their most difficult obstacle to overcome in gaining their current appointment or being appointed to more senior decision-making posts was the negative attitudes of their peers, women and men differed on their report of the other obstacles to be overcome. Women also reported the lack of a supportive professional climate, some degree of self doubt and a less than desirable level of support from family or spouse. Men reported just as many but different obstacles which they had faced. They were more likely to report that keen competition for scarce jobs made it difficult to advance, as did coming to the university from the public or private sector and the lack of support from senior administrative officers.

Sources of recognition
Women ranked all subscale measures of sources of recognition as being much more important to them than did their male peers. In

addition, the order of their importance of each source differed. Women ranked people outside the university as the most important, family, friends and other administrators next and colleagues and students last. Men ranked colleagues first and students second, family and friends third and people outside the institution last. While acknowledging they already received recognition from all of these sources, women, more than men, reported wanting more recognition than what they were receiving.

Career advancement
While women, more than men report they aspire to, prepare for, actively seek and expect to be offered an appointment to senior decision-making leadership posts within the university, half of the women who currently hold middle or senior level administrative posts report having already reached the most senior decision-making position of their career. When asked whether they believe they had already reached the most significant position in their career, more men than women agreed. Sixty-one percent of the men responded "yes" to the question. Fifty-one percent of the women agreed. Nearly half of the women reported that they had already reached the most significant position in their career and didn't appear to be considering promotion. The reasons given for not seeking or anticipating further advancement were, in the first instance, similar. Women and men in this category reported that their source of personal and professional satisfaction lay elsewhere in the university. Some strongly preferred teaching, others research. In addition many women and men reported that "enough is enough" and they didn't want any more administrative responsibilities. For women, the professional climate was not compelling and the personal costs were too high. For men, the lack of resources and poor morale in the university produced a different kind of chilly climate for administrators.

When asked if they expect to be promoted, significant gender differences appeared. Forty-three percent of women expect to be promoted to a higher administrative office. Only thirty-one percent of the men held the same expectation.

No differences were found on the measure of preparedness to move to another institution in order to be appointed to a more significant position. Data indicate that people who are prepared to accept senior administrative appointments are also prepared to relocate, if necessary, to take up such an appointment.

While women are crafters of their own career, they work for and expect appointment to more senior decision-making positions, even if it means relocation. Nearly half of the women, many of whom are now at the decanal level, believe their responsibilities for administrative leadership have peaked before assuming senior decision-making posts. Their reported withdrawal from administrative leadership at a senior level merits careful follow-up.

Varied Progress in the Presence of Exemplars

Statistical reports documenting the relatively low to moderate numbers of women in mid and senior level administrative positions, in general, often mask the fact that the progress towards an equal partnership is much more varied than it would appear. While it is a fact that some institutions have few, if any, women in senior decision-making capacities, other institutions have more than 30% of their senior administrative posts currently filled by women. The appointment of women in these "exemplar" institutions merits study. It is entirely possible that the conditions or factors which are most conducive to achieving an equal partnership in the academy are conditions which have yet to be named or understood.

Not Just a Question of Numbers

The urgent need to appoint women to senior decision-making positions is not merely a question of numerical balance. It is, more precisely, the need to diversify and strengthen the leadership of the academy through the appointment of women who will, by virtue of their own life experience, embrace the experience and knowledge of women, as well as men.

As is the case with the university's ability to mount and sustain academic programmes, sufficient numbers of women are needed to generate change in institutional policies and practices, in who is admitted to the academy, what is taught, the methodologies of teaching and learning, as well as the definition of questions which excite the mind and warrant investigation.

Conclusions: Strategies for Action

Venues for sharing knowledge and experience
At this point when the numbers of women in mid and senior level administrative posts are still moderately low, it is important to build networks which provide for inter-institutional and inter-disciplinary exchange of knowledge and experience.

Moving from debate to dialogue
The findings of these studies which indicate that the perceptions and experience of women and men are more similar than different , particularly when the level of administrative post is taken into account, should bring about a reconsideration of the often divisive we/they stances of the past. Approaches to generating higher levels of gender awareness need to be explored to dispel myths and find ways to legitimate diversity at all levels of decision-making in the academy.

Building the connection between the advancement of women and the advancement of the institution
It is in the interest of women and universities that the criteria for appointment to leadership positions specifically indicate the

skills and experience from which to speak to and guide the institution through the broader social transformations. This is an important attribute whether the leader is female or male. However, if persons most likely to be appointed to senior decision-making positions, now and in the next decade, need this knowledge and skill, then women should continue to ensure, through continuing professional education, that they are best able to make this kind of contribution. In a competition for appointment, whether the process itself is formal or informal, sought after or not, the advantage will go to the person who can lead the institution through these troubled times and leave it stronger than it was before.

The University Curriculum, Law and Gender

Henrietta Mensa-Bonsu
University of Ghana, Legon, Ghana

Introduction

The realization that tertiary education for women is the cornerstone for the advancement of their equality has been slow in coming. In the developing world, strategies for improving the status of women have placed emphasis on economic empowerment because that reflects the needs of the majority of women who are, in the main, illiterate. Even when attention has been focused on female education, the emphasis has been on primary education to which many girl-children do not even have access.[1] Attention to the needs of the illiterate majority, however, has meant that little of it has been paid to the requirements of those not in that class, but who equally need empowerment of a different kind. Thus, this emphasis on the economic empowerment of the majority has ensured an absence of the appropriate intellectual class to lead the movement.

The relevance and importance of recent proposals on the need to involve women in the policy and decision-making levels of society, as advocated by the Draft Beijing Platform for Action,[2] must be read against such a background. The recognition that the progress of women in developing countries is linked with the number of women in high policy and decision-making levels has, however, revealed the yawning gap between advocating an ideal, and the resources needed to translate this into reality. In many of the developing countries, the need to involve women at such levels has been felt, but the real issue is where to find the calibre of trained female personnel able to discharge the functions that are incidental to high-ranking positions, since years of legal and social discrimination have made it impossible for women to remain in school long enough

53

to obtain higher levels of training. Without the highly trained cadre of women able and willing to fill those high-level decision-making positions, no government, with the best will in the world, could grant to women those kinds of positions.

Another facet of the problem of the absence of highly-educated women is the fact that there is a lack of well-trained leadership to push the women's agenda. The lack of local leadership is a serious problem for any group, since serious issues can be dismissively treated, or trivialized merely because the local leadership is unable to marshal locally-relevant arguments to direct attention to complaints identified. Without appropriate leadership, the Women's Movement has often had to operate under the supervision of males - a fact which negates its very essence. These males, though often well-intentioned, have been willing to develop some initiatives, but have, in the main, succeeded in creating palliatives rather than realistic cures for some of the ills identified. Worse still is the fact that in some developing countries, gender issues have become the preserve of those who would exploit them for political self-aggrandizement, rather that of those with a real commitment to improve the lot of women. This situation has ensured that only those activities that are politically palatable are given the necessary support, thus sacrificing real improvement for politically visible initiatives. Can women themselves be empowered to take charge of their own affairs without the undue politicization which has hampered efforts for real progress on this front?

The move to target tertiary education for females is therefore a necessary intervention at this point in time. However, this effort must move beyond pointing out inequality, in terms of female access to educational facilities, to the substance of the training available in those institutions. It is not uncommon to find that some of the female enemies of the Women's Movement are to be found even in the instructor-class of tertiary institutions. These women, highly influential as they are in terms of their impact on future generations of students, can (and do) harm the cause of women. This they do, not only by putting down the concerns of women, but also by co-operating with those who would deflect criticism of their discriminatory policies by acts of tokenism. Thus, despite efforts to increase the numbers of educated females, there has been no visible change in the image of women in many societies. This situation may indeed be a reflection of the fact that the wrong questions may have been asked up to now, and so changing the focus from formal access to gender-sensitive university curricula could not have come at a better time.

University Education

The strategy to target issues of education at the university level involves a multi-pronged effort. Included in the list of matters needing attention are: increasing female access to tertiary level education; improvement of facilities for training females as academic staff of universities; re-orientation of teaching staff of universities - both male and female; re-examining curricula towards making the disciplines more gender-oriented; and the development of specific courses that address gender-related issues.

Increasing access of females to tertiary education continues to be an important consideration, since most institutional positions involving the formulation of policy require higher levels of educational attainment. Where the numbers of females applying to university institutions continue to be less than one-quarter of the total number of applicants, there is a clear indication that there is a need to adopt intervention mechanisms. The solution to this problem, however, is not one that admits of easy answers since applicants to tertiary institutions are derived from a pool of those trained in the second-cycle institutions. These second-cycle institutions are, in turn, fed by the primary levels where the problems of low female-enrolment and retention rates begin the process of low female numbers in the educational system.[3] Therefore, whatever measures are adopted must flow right through the system to address the problems from the root, though a conscious effort must be made not to let them end at those low levels.

In addition to increasing access for females generally, there must be a progression towards increasing the numbers of female academic staff in the tertiary institutions. Apart from the role-modelling effect that this would have, gender issues within the academic arena would also be brought to the fore for eventual resolution. This is because many institutions unconsciously retain an intensely male ambience which is not hospitable to females despite the fact of increasing numbers of females in the instructor class. The University of Ghana provides a good illustration of this point. For instance, the contracts between the academic staff and the University of Ghana, in a culture that puts a premium on female fertility, do not contain any provisions for Maternity Leave. Therefore the institution has had recourse to the provisions of the Labour Decree (i.e. the general law of the land) in granting maternity leave to pregnant female academic staff. The recourse to the general law of the land represents a progressive attitude of the university administration towards female staff. Were there not such a progressive attitude towards the interpretation of the terms and conditions of service of female staff members, the issue of whether pregnant female academic staff were entitled to Maternity Leave, not provided by their contracts of employment, might have had to be settled by litigation. Clearly, the absence of such provision is a relic of by-gone days when very few academics were female, or in the child-bearing age-group. Yet it is precisely such matters that may have a discouraging effect on women who would have chosen academic careers but do not pursue that path in the belief that the academic atmosphere is hostile to them.

In addition to improving the numbers of women opting for academic life, those already pursuing such careers may have to be targeted for self-improvement schemes so as to be prepared for higher levels of responsibility within their own institutions. Such programmes also have to sensitize women concerning the need to improve gender-awareness inside their own institutions, as well as to introduce gender issues to their own students. By creating the opportunity for women in academia to also aspire to policy and decision-making levels in their own institutions, they would increase the visibility of women in those institutions, and help in fostering an environment that females would not find inhospitable. An institution with such a female-friendly environment would also do much towards improving the confidence of women who are trained therein.

There is clearly a major stumbling block in this area of female access to policy-making positions within their own academic institutions - a situation which requires attention. The issue is this: many offices in academia are elective in nature and often open only to very senior academics of those institutions. This presents two major problems: the numbers of females in the pool of senior academics, and the number of constituents willing to elect a female office-holder. These two factors are important in determining whether a female can ever hold such office. The first problem may resolve itself with time when sufficient numbers of female academics will have worked themselves up the academic ladder into senior positions. The second does not admit of such easy resolution. What can be done about such a situation is not a simple issue since one ought not to sacrifice easily democratic ideals for the attainment of other ends. Perhaps more females could be considered for appointive positions so as to give them an opportunity to prove their mettle to otherwise sceptical colleagues, and eventually command enough respect from them to earn their vote for elective offices. Perhaps other initiatives that would guarantee exposure to programmes that teach self-assertiveness might develop a cadre of self-assured women who would inspire the necessary confidence in their male colleagues. No doubt a programme, such as the UNITWIN/UNESCO Chairs programme may do this if it succeeds in providing management training for a critical mass of women academics and administrators.

The Law

The teaching, study and practice of Law has, in the past, been a male preserve. Until the late 1970s, the Faculty of Law of the University of Ghana had very few females. This fact was not the result of active discriminatory policies at the institutional level, but a function of the pyramidal structure of education in Ghana.[4] With very few people qualifying to enter the university as a whole,[5] it is no surprise that those who qualify to pursue Law as a discipline are also few in number. Yet even within this small number, the female numbers did tend to be on the low side. In 1973, there were only 30 female lawyers in Ghana as against 210 males.[6] Since then, the numbers have improved somewhat. A look at the female enrolment for the last twenty years (i.e. 1975-1994) at the Faculty of Law at the University of Ghana illustrates the point:

1975	8	of	82		1985	16	of	79
1976	8	of	79		1986	22	of	67
1977	14	of	70		1987	14	of	78
1978	7	of	55		1988	33	of	72
1979	10	of	67		1989	22	of	74
1980	14	of	74		1990	40	of	75
1981	11	of	76		1991	33	of	81
1982	21	of	83		1992	22	of	76
1983	-	-	-[7]		1993	33	of	83
1984	20	of	75		1994	35	of	78

The figures indicate that there has been marked improvement in the enrolment level since the 1970s when it was often in the single digit range. Indeed, from the figures, it is clear that in the 1990/91 academic year, more females than males enrolled in the Faculty. However it is to be observed that until the late 1980s, the percentages were very low. The improvement is not attributable to any intervention mechanisms put in place, but possibly, to changing public perceptions of the openings that are available in the profession for women. As well, advocacy has social visibility so this, along with commitment to women's issues by females lawyers in Ghana, has enhanced their profile.

Despite the improvement in the number of female students, however, the male-female ratio is still a far cry from what it should be, and therefore the profession retains a very male-oriented outlook. It is quite usual to find people addressing the female judges as "My Lord", and quite usual to find women judges acknowledging that form of address as the proper one.[8] Therefore it is clear that more needs to change than the mere fact of a lop-sided male-female ratio. This is where the substance of the courses begins to matter.

The Law Curriculum

The current push towards examining university curricula is also a logical progression from improving formal access of females to "substantive" access as represented by the content of the training received by students. In a discipline such as Law, rules that appear innocuous can, in fact, be the basis for gender-based discrimination. In the same way, philosophical attitudes of a bygone era may continue to hold sway in the legal arena and legitimize discriminatory practices merely because instructors may not have been sensitized in a different direction. Therefore curricula developed upon those philosophical notions also need to be reviewed in order to make them responsive to current ideas. This is vital since, in the main, the attitudes of the policy-makers of the twenty-first century are being shaped at the current time in tertiary institutions. Whether gender issues might be recognized as serious issues for the whole society or not could depend to a considerable extent upon the kind of exposure that students in universities are receiving at the present time.

The need to revise the curriculum to include gender-oriented courses is now receiving attention in many Law Schools, and Ghana is no different in this regard. In order to sensitize the new generation of Ghanaian lawyers to the relevant issues, a course entitled 'Gender and the Law' has been developed and offered from the current 1994-1995 academic year onwards. What is interesting to note is that no one signed up for that course for the first semester, although it was advertised well in advance. Comparable figures for other new courses in their first year are as follows: Natural Resources Law =13[9] ; International Human Rights Law = 4[10] ; and Intellectual Property Law = 9[11] . It can therefore be deduced that a course on Gender and Law is not as attractive to Law students as other types of courses. The reason may be as ordinary as the fact that it does not improve the chances of employment in any particular direction, whilst the other new course offerings have the advantage of providing special skills required in particular areas of employment. If this is the reason, then it may be necessary to encourage employers of development-oriented organizations (particularly those using donor-funds) to specify gender-oriented studies as an advantage for potential applicants. The cold-shouldering of the course may however be due to a more sinister reason: the fact that the students rate the issues as disclosed by the course outline as second-rate in importance and therefore not worthy of their study time.

This first-year experience with Gender and the Law should not depress us into an attitude that a separate course on gender is perhaps not needed at the present time. Even the mere fact that there is now a whole course on offer should send the right kind of signals to students about the status of gender studies, and this in turn, is bound to affect perceptions of the relevance of such issues. There are, however, other serious lessons to be learnt from this experience. It may in fact be indicative of the need to change strategy so as to cultivate student interest in gender studies. Perhaps the introduction of a separate course on gender should have been linked with a fresh examination of existing material in the light of emerging gender issues, so that the appetite of students would have been whetted for these studies.

The point being made above is that the cold reception of the course on gender underlines ‘the need to mainstream gender studies so that persons trained in the law would have exposure to alternative thinking on particular legal issues whether or not they opt for specific gender studies. The impact that such exposure could have on the application of the laws as they exist at the moment would go a long way towards raising the sensitivity of the law to issues of gender. An instance illustrating the importance of the alternative interpretation can be found in two distinct interpretations of a particular rule - so that it either gets reinforcement as a necessary measure for enhancing women's rights, or is undermined as reinforcing traditional attitudes inimical to women. The Labour Decree of Ghana[12] provides that women should not do night work or underground work in industry. The author contends that this is a discriminatory rule that might prevent some women from doing work they wish to do, or that might affect their career prospects in terms of advancement to supervisory grades.[13] Another writer lists the provision as one of the protective pieces of legislation "to ensure that women do not undertake hazardous work such as underground mining work..."[14] Clearly these two interpretations of the relevance of the provision are at variance with each other. It is, however, likely, that the second interpretation represents current legislative thinking on the subject. If indeed it does militate against the enjoyment of equal treatment in employment for some women, whatever the nature of the protection it intended to afford to this group, it is inimical to women's right to the employment of their choice. What is wrong with a woman wanting to be a miner? Is not this desire to prevent women from doing "hazardous" work a reflection of the paternalistic attitudes which have led to the exclusion of women from the enjoyment of certain human rights? Whatever the merits of either view, it is clear that exposure to alternative thinking on existing material can make a lot of difference regarding the attitudes of future lawyers to gender issues.

Orientation of Professors

Mainstreaming gender studies also means adopting a different pedagogical approach to instruction. This in turn requires sensitizing and re-orientating academic instructors in the universities to the gender dimensions of the courses that they teach. Where instructing personnel are committed to espousing "black-letter rules" and nothing more, their students are not likely to be exposed to alternate thinking on relevant legal issues. In this regard, the approach perceived to be best suited to mainstreaming gender issues is borrowed from Roger Brownsword.[15] Although he was putting forward a prescription for the teaching of Contract Law, his ideas are nevertheless useful to any instructor who would expose students to new ways of thinking. He indicates that the line of first-order inquiry concerns "formal normative materials".

a) Exegetical questions: What do the statutes and precedents provide? (This is where black-letter inquiry begins and ends.)
b) Interpretative questions: What is the deep structure of the materials? What values (similarly what centology) is [sic] pre-supposed by the materials?
c) Evaluative Questions: Are the materials effective in serving their regulatory ends and are those ends legitimate?...
d) Historical-descriptive questions: What has been the historical development of the materials?
e) Explanatory questions: How do we account for the enactment of such and such a provision (or failure) to enact such a provision or how do we explain some doctrinal development or transformation?"

When such an approach is adopted, the different possibilities would be exposed and the students made to question views and interpretations based on conventional wisdom. This approach would also enable an instructor, who so wishes, to introduce gender-oriented considerations into the material under discussion. How can an instructor do this, when he or she knows of no other approach? The inescapable conclusion is that academic instructors need to be introduced to new ideas through training programmes of different kinds. When such opportunities become available, they should not be limited to females only, as has been the practice with many gender-related programmes. Since there are more male instructors that female ones, they consequently stand to influence more minds than the females can reach.

Other Issues of Gender and the Law

Problems of the legal system range from little issues to big ones. Unimportant though some appear to be, they are still indicative of deep-seated problems arising from cultural attitudes. Thus, a systematic exposure to gender issues would be necessary to rectify these. For instance, statutory interpretation rules provide that "In an enactment, words importing the male sex include females and words importing the female sex include males."[16] This is an oft-quoted provision when the male gender is used in legal circles. However, in actual fact, there is no statutory provision intended for both males and females, which uses the feminine gender. On all the occasions on which the feminine gender is used, the provisions are specifically aimed at females.[17] The statutory provision thus recognizes the equality of the genders but the practice, informed by societal attitudes, maintains a steadfast position on the appropriateness of subsuming the feminine under the masculine, but never the other way round. The result of this is to exemplify the attitude in the law that "the greater includes the lesser." How, then, can one pretend to regard both genders as being of equal status?

There are, however, more serious problems regarding the structure of the legal systems themselves that pose challenges to those who develop courses on gender. Most jurisdictions in Africa - with Ghana being no exception - operate pluralistic legal systems - either the common law, customary law and Islamic law, or the continental law of Europe, Islamic and customary law in

Anglophone, Francophone and Lusophone Africa respectively. Each system has its own peculiar attitudes which dictate the nature of the problems associated with the particular legal systems that practise them. Thus, gender studies in such pluralistic systems have to draw on the experiences of the various systems and then attempt to harmonize the rules to achieve results that are the most favourable under the circumstances.

Owing to problems of pluralism, it would seem to be of the utmost importance to stress international commitments to women's rights as contained in international instruments such as the Convention on Elimination of All Forms of Discrimination against Women. This avenue would put beyond argument the suitability (or otherwise) of particular views being advocated since they might derive most support from treaty obligations voluntarily assumed by the state in question. This means that courses on Law and Gender should make a conscious effort to acquaint students with the substance of international women's rights instruments. In addition, students must be encouraged to identify cultural bottlenecks that defeat the proper application of international instruments within the particular jurisdiction. Such cultural rules that are identified would in the future become the targets for change by those who had been exposed to gender studies. Too often, all emphasis is put on a study of the status quo as reflected by domestic legislation, and not enough on the possibilities for the future as dictated by the assumption of international commitments.

Legal Scholarship

An important ingredient in university education is scholarship. Therefore in Law , as in other areas, the importance of scholarship in promoting change should not be underrated. Research that exposes inconsistencies in legislation, double standards and unjust effects of particular rules can have real value for anyone seeking to change both the law itself and the attitudes of policy-makers. For instance, scholarly research indicating that domestic violence gets gentler treatment from the law enforcement agencies than other forms of violence, is likely to cause a re-examination of methods and other policies aimed at reducing such violence. Since other kinds of literature get treated with less seriousness, scholarly publications do make a difference. The battle to promote gender-sensitivity must therefore not exclude legal scholarship.

Promoting legal scholarship has funding implications both for the conduct of research and for its publication. Field research is expensive but necessary if authentic information is to be acquired. Therefore, avenues for funding gender-related legal research must be made available so that deserving research projects can be supported. Currently, only Science and Technology-related research have priority in terms of funding owing to scarce national resources. Without recourse to non-national sources of funding, very little primary legal research of any kind can be done. Publication of research findings is the logical step after funding has been provided for fieldwork. There are very few journals available for legal publications in the developing countries. Of this number, many are committed to International Law and therefore all other areas must compete for the available space. It is thus imperative that a journal devoted to women's issues be established to make it possible for those who engage in gender-related research to publish such research. Apart from circumventing editorial prejudices, this would be an added incentive for legal scholars to undertake this type of research since there would be an increased likelihood of publication.

Conclusion

The foregoing discussion has attempted to isolate issues that can promote gender equality by focusing on university policies and curricula. The issues range from increasing formal access to university education for women, through promoting substantive access by emphasizing gender studies, to improving the scholarship basis for these. What is clear, certainly from the

Ghanaian experience, is that it is not enough to develop specific courses on gender, without putting other initiatives in place as well.

Notes

1. *Draft African Platform for Action*; Fifth African Regional Conference on Women, Dakar, 1994.

2. Section IV. G. par. 94.

3. For instance the drop-out rate of the cohort of children who entered class 1 and completed J.S.S. 3 in 1991/1992 was 48.6% i.e. 43% male and 55% female. (Revised Ghana National Population Policy Action Plan vol. III p. 2. National Population Council: 1994).

4. The education model in Ghana is pyramidal in nature (i.e. a large base and a thin apex) because only a small proportion of those who enter school in any particular year get into the secondary schools, and an even smaller percentage of that number end up in the tertiary institutions.

5. The "guesstimate" puts the figure at about 1% of the cohort of children who enter class 1.

6. *Report of Manpower Survey*, Manpower Division, Ministry of Finance and Economic Planning. (unpublished).

7. There was no intake as a result of a year-long closure of the University after several student demonstrations.

8. A 1965 editorial 'joke' is instructive of this point. The comment pertained to the proper form of address for females on the Bench and at the Bar. Now that we have been obliged to recognize that the profession is de-sexual (or is it bi-sexual), and not mono/unisexual, it seems we are henceforth permitted to say "Her Worship", "Her Honour" and "Her Ladyship". ... But what about "Barristress-at-Law" and "Solicitress"? Do we have these professionals also? Or our lady "brothers" do not wish to carry their battle for equality that far?
    'Bit & Pieces' [1965] *Current Cases* vol. 6 p. iii. The Editor at the time is now a Supreme Court judge.

9. 1989/90.

10. 1991/92.
11. 1992/93.

12. *N.L.C.D.157 of 1967, Section 41*

13. *The Subtle Effects of Legislation on Women and Childbearing* Report of the Ghana National Conference on Population and Development. vol. II (Population Impact Project: 1986)

14. Ofori-Boateng, Sabina. *Enhancing Gender Research and Training. The Research and Training Needs of Policy-makers: Law-Making Policy.* Paper presented at International Workshop on Gender Research and Training, Accra, February 1995. (The author is the Director, Legislative Drafting Section, Ministry of Justice, Ghana.)

15. Birks, Peter (ed.) "Teaching Contract: A Liberal Agenda." *Examining The Law Syllabus* p. 42-45 (Oxford University Press: 1992)

16. Section 26(1) Interpretation Act 1960 (C.A.4).y

17. These are usually sexual offences and offences of procuration, which can be committed only in respect of females.

Women and Development: Perspectives and Challenges within the University Curriculum

Maria Inácia D'Avilo-Neto
With the collaboration of **Christiana A. Baptista**
and Renata Calicchio
Federal University of Rio de Janeiro, Brazil

Introduction

In 1992, the Federal University of Rio de Janeiro, the largest public university in Brazil,[1] held a meeting to follow-up the 1992 United Nations Conference on Environment and Development (UNCED)(UFRJ). Sponsored by the federal government, this meeting brought together scientists and researchers from both Brazil and abroad to study environmental and development issues.

As part of the programme,[2] a seminar was suggested on the theme of **Gender, Environment and Development** in order to promote Agenda 21 which targets the inclusion of a gender dimension in any debate on these subjects.[3] The initial reaction of the organizing committee was negative, and the seminar proposal was turned down on the grounds that its theme was not pertinent to environmental and development questions. Fortunately, persuasion prevailed and, despite limited resources, the seminar took place in May 1992 with strong participatory support. However, resistance was evident in many quarters. Thus the experience itself provided an opportunity for serious reflection on the theme chosen.[4]

At the UFRJ, several groups deal with questions related to gender and society. This is equally true for other universities in the Latin American region. Considerable research has been done on a wide variety of topics covering women in the work force, their health and nutrition, fertility and reproduction, genetic engineering, sociolinguistic patterns, socialization practices, stereotyping,

69

empowerment and exposure to violence. These studies have dealt with both urban and rural contexts and embraced many academic fields, inter alia, Philosophy, Sociology, Economics, Medicine and Social Ecology. Research funding is obtained from different sources, and there is now an established magazine for feminist issues.

This indicates a rising interest in gender amongst the academic community, as is witnessed by the organization of meetings, visiting professorships, research for Master's and doctoral theses, prolific publications and growing international exchanges between Brazil and other countries.

At the same time, the number of women enrolled in university is increasing every year. For example, only 30% of students were women in 1965. Today, they make up 52% of all enrolments in the 20-24 age bracket.[5]

Yet, despite this impressive volume of research and teaching on the condition of women, and particularly on their social and economic status, the academic milieu still manifests a reluctance to tackle this subject. This not only recalls our experience with regard to the 1992 seminar, but is also evident in the design of development projects which tend to omit the gender dimension altogether.

This chapter seeks to analyse a complex situation, since recognition of women's equality is the necessary starting point for including their specific interests in every field of education and of professional life.

Studies on Women in the Academy

Many researchers, such as Maria Mies a well-known German feminist and former teacher at the University of Cologne, and Jalna Hanmer of the University of Bradford, United Kingdom, have perceived this to be an ambiguous problem.[6] It is essential that Women's Studies, as a field of academic education, should be seen as part of a wider perspective so as to ensure a coherent vision of gender. Unless this is the case, the academic approach can be isolated from issues related to social policy. It is thus necessary to ally practice and theory since the obstacles to the gender dimension are numerous.[7]

Certain academics, including Maria Mies, Susan Harding[8] Evelyn Fox Keller[9] and Carolyn Merchant,[10] have even proposed a "feminist epistemology" to balance the dominance of the male or patriarchal perspective in the search for new knowledge. However, for Jacqueline Feldman, science (i.e. knowledge) is neither male nor female and so this criticism does not really address the reality of abstract thought - a view expressed in her paper on pluridisciplinary androgyny.[11] Feldman also contends that science can be ideological. This idea is evident in Habermas' texts relating method and science to ideology and also can be perceived in the observations of scientists when communicating information on a particular discovery. A typical example is the debate on possible sexual differences in relation to the human brain.[12]

However, this chapter is not concerned with the male or female nature of knowledge. Our primary concern is the assurance of the gender dimension in all academic activity - research, teaching and training. In this respect, gender goes beyond a disciplinary discussion such as Women's Studies. Rather, it should be considered as being transversal to all fields. In this way, the true equality of women can be promoted - in the academic and other professions and in the overall development process.

Women and Development: Key Issues

The Brazilian Context
In order to design a university curriculum in Development Studies which includes the gender dimension, it is first necessary

to reflect on the actual concept of development. Then its application in various contexts can be more effective.

Brazil has a population of some 150 million - of whom approximately 17% of adults (aged 15 years and above) are illiterate. More than half of those entering basic education do not manage to finish the first grade, and only about 11% of the 18 - 22 age group are enrolled in higher education. Clearly, access to education is far from equal and there is strong emphasis on economic growth without due concern for social development.

Nevertheless, over the past decade, women's overall access to education has generally improved. Their literacy level has increased and, in higher education, they now constitute about 52% of all enrolments.

However, a closer study of these statistics shows that certain segments of the population are disadvantaged. Amongst those whose formal education stops after the first grade, 40% are of indigenous origin. In comparison, this situation is true for only 20% of white females. Geographical trends also show inequalities since 40% of such people live in the more remote Northeastern area while their presence in the South East (a more developed region) is notably reduced. These figures illustrate the challenges facing Brazilian education as well as the general development pattern of the country.

An analysis of the development concept raises a number of key questions related to women:
- have they received proper consideration in this area?
- how can studies on women contribute to a better development process?
- can closer collaboration amongst the various disciplines related to development improve the condition of women?

While certain academics doubt the value of Women's Studies, this field can stimulate reflection on what may be called "social asymmetries" which demonstrate the complex and often conflicting issues in countries such as Brazil. While development issues can be viewed from the North and South standpoints as well as from traditional or innovative positions, the overall aim is a more just and equal society, and the feminist voice is an important source of criticism, especially in the developing world. A good example is the analysis of the "prudent subsistence and poverty" question made by the well-known Indian feminist Vandana Shiva. She demonstrated that traditional subsistence cultures have been eliminated in several regions because development has been based on Western (or Northern) models. This occurred in Africa where tribes were relocated to accommodate mechanized agriculture. The Amazon met the same fate since its native rubber workers had to leave to create pasture land for cattle. As a result, the livelihood of many families was destroyed. Can this be termed "development" when tribal groups are decimated by hunger, (which was the consequence in Africa), and when rural populations are forced into urban poverty where women and girls must become prostitutes to survive? Such disasters are often used to emphasize ill-conceived development models and co-operation projects driven by the North.

Moreover, I have witnessed widespread silence as to what feminism proposes for women from developing countries. There exists a major erroneous premise on the part of Western-style feminism - namely, that all women in all societies suffer from oppression in one form or another and so their demands can all be grouped in one single agenda. Aminate Traore, the African sociologist and feminist says: "Since the body is the main concern for Western feminists, when they look at Africa, they are always concerned over mutilation, polygamy and multiple maternity. The body's integrity goes far beyond these issues. No feminist asks what we really want. If we said we wanted more children, it would be a catastrophe ...." She also argues that certain development projects aimed at bolstering women's incomes, such as cottage industries and horticulture, have succeeded only in increasing their already heavy workload.[13]

I would add that women in Latin America have one of the lowest percentages of free or leisure time in the world. There are two reasons for this: firstly, no economic or social structure in any country has ever given adequate visibility to domestic labour (including the care and education of children); secondly, women from different societies have different feelings and aspirations regarding the value of this type of work. Hence, they view the functions of wife, mother and homemaker in very different ways.

Women's Expectations
So, feminism which does not really recognize the priorities of women from various cultures is as pernicious as the North-driven development model which imposes technological solutions without considering local culture and knowledge. Basically, both seek to dominate and leave no room for **difference**. This is a contradictory situation since, above all, feminism demands recognition for the right of women to be different from men.

It thus becomes possible to reformulate our previous questions:
- is there an adequate development model for women?
- does a specific culture justify a specific development model?

Development models should target the well-being of both men and women so that their relations may be correctly balanced and so that each can pursue personal fulfilment. The inclusion of women in farming or in small-scale industry is not the main issue. Rather, the key is the quality of their life - that is, whether women are able to benefit from culture, from education and from other activities which lead to their equality. Their freedom is threatened not only by male oppression but also by social, economic or racial injustice. Furthermore, oppression can come from entities such as international bodies, multi-nationals and even from powerful NGOs for women.

In this respect, it is interesting to examine the recommendations of the World Social Summit (Copenhagen 1995) which link demographic growth with the education of women and youth.

This could be a potentially dangerous linkage if women were to be held solely responsible for the birth rate, due to their lack of education or inability to mobilize the necessary resources to control population. This shifts the responsibility for a possible global catastrophe - unfairly - to women alone and ignores the other important actors involved, notably men and governments.

In Brazil, the birth rate has decreased in the last decade and the average age of the population has become older. These trends are recommended by international organizations. Yet, when the income distribution of the population is studied, 30% remain as poor as they were twenty years ago. For some, their income has even decreased. Furthermore, only 10% of this group appear to have become better off. This situation is more or less typical of the overpopulation phenomenon affecting large cities. In the Southeastern area of the country where Rio de Janeiro (pop. 12 million) and Sao Paulo (pop. 17 million) are located, migration from rural areas has greatly increased. The search for better opportunities has gradually turned into frustration. Underprivileged women, whose migration rate is already higher than men's, have abandoned their own domestic and agricultural work to take jobs in the cities, where almost all domestic workers come from rural areas or poorer urban centres. There is a new problem emerging - that of violence against women where the perpetrators are almost always men from the families involved. This is nation-wide and has mobilized the support of police (notably the increased involvement of women officers in this task) as well as of academic groups interested in researching its origins.

Vandana Shiva made the following comment on the failure of actions planned by the United Nations Decade for Women in favour of those from the so-called Third World:

"Women's insufficient participation in development has not been the cause of women's growing underdevelopment. This results from their forced and asymmetrical participation in a process for which they have paid the cost but have been excluded from the benefits."[14]

International experts continue to insist that the problem of development affects humankind as a whole, based on the premise that growth in the GNP of a country must be analyzed in terms of its benefits for all social groups. However, in fact, Shiva goes on to stress the concept of "bad development" which:

> "... is usually referred to as economic growth and is measured by the Gross Domestic Product .... As a measure of growth, it is pretty much useless .... Many goods and services it measures do not benefit persons, but merely indicate how much the following are growing: expenditures for pollution and crime control, waste .... All is accounted for. ... with few exceptions, women's relative access to economic resources, inputs and employment have decreased: their work load has increased, and their relative and even absolute health conditions and nutritional and educational status have declined."[15]

Thus, the Indian feminist believes that women have failed to benefit from a major portion of the development process which is little more than a poor replica of colonialism.

The predominance of male models in most societies, even in the most advanced ones, continues to intrigue those experts studying the cultural development process. This raises the old issue of the oppressor and the oppressed, the appropriation of one by the other in the name of gender rather than in the name of social or economic development. Without doubt, the power relationship is at the root of this problem - and, as is the case with all power relationships, they are asymmetrical, fated and even regarded fatalistically by those involved. This is because they are based on sexism, a term coined by the French writer, Colette, to designate what she described as "a sex-sign entity" - that is, the appropriation of an object called "woman".[16]

It is clear, even for the more naive, that the issue of women in the development process is far from being solved either by the specific agents concerned or by the agencies which promote this goal - whether they be domestic or international. This is the least camouflaged of all forms of discrimination which renders it extremely difficult to confront. Broader development models frequently encounter the real cultural obstacle to change which can be found in all societies - namely, this asymmetrical power relationship which can become too easily accepted if tasks as diverse as domestic and family duties, the teaching of values and lowly-paid jobs are essentially seen to be "women's work".

At the same time, it is true that certain proposals for social and cultural development have focused attention on pertinent facts related to women's inequality: fewer educational opportunities, lower wages for the same work, disrespect for women's rights, physical and sexual abuse, and stereo-typed images in the media or in the school curriculum. In addition, the whole area of contraception and genetic engineering has opened a heated debate which has offended the dignity of many women. Most of these proposals have fallen far short of producing cultural policies for global well-being, and especially the actual elimination of sexual discrimination. This was very clearly demonstrated by the great diversities between North and South at the International Conference on Population and Development (Cairo, 1994).

The arguments go beyond the socio-political dimension, and one cannot ascribe this oppression of women by men to any single political regime. Although Vandana Shiva and other feminists, such as Maria Mies, may appear to place liberals and socialists on opposite sides of the fence, the reality of the situation is less clear-cut. For example, when commenting on the Chinese revolution, Mao Tse Tung used to say that his only failure was to change the prevailing conservative attitude towards women. Complaints are numerous and have a common ring - in Cuba, in Nordic countries, amongst Lapon Indian women or the female bugres of the Pantanal, from domestic workers in Rio de Janeiro or from Left Bank intellectuals in Paris.

We might then conclude that if prejudice against women persists in various socio-political models, the same is also found in endogenous development models. Yet this might be too pessimistic and fatalistic. It would be more useful to take a closer look at the power relationships embedded in the development process, particularly as they affect women, and to examine the recommendations for a "culture of women".

Gender as a Dimension of Development
Let us again return to our two key questions: is there an adequate development model for women, and is there a specific women's culture which justifies a specific development model?

We are familiar with the concepts of endogenous development and local development which raise issues related to different cultures, regionalization and adaptation of new technologies to traditional community knowledge. We are also familiar with the criticism levelled at autocratic, "top-down" development models which exclude community participation and do not take account of their traditions or cultural values. Today, participation is the "buzz-word" which supposedly opens the doors to international aid, and human development is the term used to denote the final goal of all this participatory activity.

Throughout the 1980s, the mission of the international co-operation agencies was debated at length. Was co-operation the **transmission** of new and more advanced expertise and technology so that these may be shared by rich and poor countries alike? Or, was co-operation an act of **submission** on the part of the so-called underdeveloped countries to the supposedly more advanced?[17] This line of questioning gave rise to terms such as Eco-development and Sustainable Development.

Today at long last, the actual existence of a "culture of women" is beginning to be recognized. However, this is not as well accepted as that of other social minority groups. As Jean Collin says, "It may be significant that cultural discourse, the origins of which tend to multiply cultures and sub-cultures according to possible human groupings in time and space, has never invoked, as far as I know, the idea of a culture of men and a culture of women...."[18]

Why is this so? Firstly, I suppose, because there is an earlier and more simplistic tendency to place women alongside **nature** - in contrast with **culture** which was seen as an essentially masculine preserve. Women are assimilated into nature which is seen as instinctive, embracing and encompassing - hence the association with abnegation and reproduction. Man is the source of order, law and defence -hence his association with domination. When this issue was raised by the Eco-feminists, both in the USA and in Europe, they earned harsh criticism from other groups of feminist activists and academics in spite of their politically correct argument. To associate nature and women has been used as the ideological basis to justify the power relationship which promotes the appropriation of women by men - an argument used, inter alia, by Guillaumin. The very idea of making "natural" that which is "cultural" prevents a discussion of the social issues which involve the matter of the gender sign. For this reason, academics have preferred to replace the term "sexual identity" by "gender issues".

It is useful to ask whether, when we speak of a "feminine culture", we are not simply changing the sign? Might "culture", (as used to denote the specificity of a given group - i.e. women) have the same ideological force as that ascribed to "nature" when used in the same sense? In other words, the difference is semantic.

Françoise Collin points out this issue when discussing George Simmel's contribution to feminine culture.[19] Simmel's most profound work on the women's issue includes two articles entitled *Feminine Culture* (1902) and *From the Relative to the Absolute in the Issue of the Sexes* (1911).[20] By distinguishing between "objective" and "subjective" culture, Simmel becomes a precursor of themes held in high esteem by feminists and even by the donor community interested in women's projects. "Objective" culture includes all external forms such as art, law, customs and religion. "Subjective" culture is marked by the phenomenon of individual **participation** in the former - thereby nourishing personal growth. By proposing a new cultural space (i.e. this culture of women), Simmel maintains that objective culture is essentially masculine.[21] So, when women's movements strive to participate more in this area, they are really trying to promote their own "subjective" culture. The masculine "objective" culture is segmented and compartmentalized in character. This is foreign to women who gravitate towards that which is holistic and encompassing. A woman's existence is thus fundamentally different from that of a man. She does not compartmentalize her roles as wife, mother or daughter. Thus, Simmel holds that women's movements aim to create an independent but holistic femininity - this is the essence of the new cultural space. Moreover, he considers that this could contribute to a more egalitarian vision in education, in law, in professional life and in social behaviour.

However, this vision can be contrasted with another of Simmel's theories which is actually quite contradictory. He suggests that it may be impossible for women to make their existence objective and to express their specificity in an external manner. If this is so, they will fail to gain autonomy which can only result from recognition of their difference, their independence and their creativity.

Although the concept of a feminine culture remains problematical for Simmel, others see it in a stark and more revolutionary way. The struggle of women is likened to that of the working class which can "shake the foundations of the unconscious and destroy ideologies".[22] The world is seen in a new light ranging from the innovative views proposed by American anthropologists in the 1970s (i.e. Lamphere, Rosaldo, Chodorow et al.) to the daring vision of the contemporary existentialists such as the Canadian, Nicole Brossard, who contends that femininity is something "prior" and impossible to reduce to the man-women axis. Its essence is that of a fluidity or of a spiral - that is to say, it is something which is indivisible. This view is similar to the arguments advanced by the French thinkers, Françoise Collin and Jacques Derrida. An analogy might be the paradox of maternity where the child always maintains an indivisible link with its mother - even after the physical separation of birth. Another metaphor is the relation between the artist and his or her creation - they are forever associated. In contrast with this rather spiritual perspective, the Western world and thus its development model seem pragmatic and strategic in approach.

These remarks show that the concept of development and, particularly, that of women's development, do in fact constitute an academic discipline. Development theory must be constructed from a variety of sources and must be tested in practice - in this way, the change desired can be brought about from a solid intellectual basis.

Brazilian Women and the University - the Case of the UFRJ

The UFRJ has 2,210 male and 1,430 female professors. The latter's proportion (i.e. 39.2%) is slightly higher than the Brazilian average where women hold about one third of all such posts. About 11% of the population between the ages of 20 and 24 accede to university education. At the UFRJ, (as in many other Brazilian universities), the majority of females enrol in the Humanities and fields such as Psychology, Sociology, Education and in professional domains such as Nursing - a traditionally female precinct. At the present time, more women students are enrolled than men overall.

Women continue to study the Humanities and artistic fields (where they outnumber men by 2:1) and they also dominate in the health sciences, even in Medicine. Only in Engineering and other scientific and technological areas are women much less prominent - for example, 39.4% in Chemistry and just 14.9% in the Engineering School. Women's enrolment in Mathematics and Environmental Sciences is a little better and there is a fair gender balance in Law, Economics and Public Administration. These facts demonstrate a changing situation as women are advancing to occupy more posts in the academic profession and to enrol in disciplines previously dominated by men.

Perspectives for a New Curriculum in Development and Environmental Studies

In Brazil, an educational council linked to the Ministry of Education approves the curricula for degrees. Every discipline has a basic curriculum which must be taught. Some go back nearly thirty years, which is the case for Psychology. While certain institutions are trying to adapt the curriculum to reflect the "new social reality", the quality achieved is uneven. Degrees in the so-called Exact Sciences are becoming more multi-disciplinary due to the inclusion of many other subjects in their structure.

The general result is rather poor, and little attention has been paid to retraining the professoriate for the new approaches needed to address the complex social and cultural problems in today's world. These require an inter-disciplinary vision, not just a mix of different courses. Furthermore, professors are obliged to provide education which will promote development and environmental conservation, as well as the over-arching objectives of peace and tolerance.

Today, the issues related to development and the environment are crucial and require inter-disciplinary approaches - that is, new teaching and learning strategies that reflect the changing vision of the world. Associating women with this new approach remains a challenge, but the area of post-graduate studies, which can be more innovative, offers some hope in this respect. Newly created

Master's and doctoral degrees should definitely take up this challenge.

At the UFRJ, we created a course entitled EICOS which involves inter-disciplinary studies of communities via a programme in Social Ecology.[23] It tackles the cultural, social and ecological dimensions of development and is taught at the Master's level. One central area of research is the link between gender, environment and development. Students choosing this area then focus on topics such as Eco-feminism and the representation of women in Brazilian society. For example, one component of our course on women deals with the perceptions of professors and students regarding their own career choices.[24] This leads to a better understanding of professions which have become labelled "male" and "female". A participative teaching methodology is favoured, though the traditional quantitative and statistical approaches are still included. The course is based in the Institute of Psychology but attracts students from Geography, Biology, the Social Sciences and Environmental Engineering. For this reason, we consider it to be extremely valuable.[25]

Programmes such as this are attempting to present a more critical vision of the world via the curriculum. As this approach is new, there is a process of trial and error but efforts must continue. Another example is a Diploma in Environmental Studies which includes topics ranging from environmental rights to nuclear power. It is possible to design a framework which can accommodate these subjects. Of course, there will be some debate on various managerial aspects of such programmes. Should they be post-graduate only? In which faculty should they be located? Which academic should be the programme leader? These are normal queries and must be resolved amongst the professors who are actually involved in inter-disciplinary research. This approach seeks to reflect the complex nature of the world and to teach students how to tackle its serious problems. Michael Apple of Wisconsin University has criticized the way in which school students are taught compartmentalized knowledge which does not show the true overlap and interaction between disciplines.[26] University teaching should not follow this pattern. Instead, it should encourage greater exchange between areas of expertise. For example, Architecture and Engineering would contribute better to urbanization if there were dialogue with sociologists, anthropologists and psychologists. Many such fields could benefit from this approach at both the theoretical and practical levels.

The Challenges of Change

An academic study of women in relation to environment and development should have, as its ultimate aim, their enhanced social insertion in their respective communities. Thus, the curriculum itself is but one element of innovation. Other areas to be considered are the values to be promoted in such a course, the methodology chosen, the major concepts to be analysed and the inclusion of the gender dimension. This approach should include a review of knowledge and technology imported from elsewhere, and which are inadequate to help resolve the problems at hand.

Taken together, these components lead us to formulate two basic premises in relation to the concept of environment and development:

- that environment cannot be considered as an isolated entity but as part of a community's culture. It is an interaction between the socio-cultural sphere (generated by Man) and nature;
- that so-called development activities (whether they target the preservation of the environment or the optimal management of environmental change) cannot be dissociated from Man's relationship with these nor from the cultural dynamics involved.

Changing Values

This is another sensitive area where the values of the researcher (i.e. his/her own ethics in relation to development) must be clearly defined. So often already, relations between North and South are called into question because alien expertise is applied without respect for the values and traditions of local cultures.

To place Man at the centre of the development process means more than simply calling this "sustainable human development". It means that the development process must serve humankind as a whole. Moreover, this in not just an abstract idea as real people (i.e. men and women) are involved here. They belong to specific communities with specific characteristics - equality depends on recognition of their right to be different.

Methodological Changes
Community participation in the development process is a fundamental tenet for all donor agencies, including NGOs. This has led to a methodological change with the result that development research must now be "participatory" or "action-oriented". However, this type of investigation has placed too much emphasis on the value of the raw data given to researchers. Some have reached a state of virtual paralysis, believing that "participatory research" prohibits any interpretation of the material provided by the persons studied. Consequently, the construction of valid Sociological or Psychological theory has been impeded. However, researchers cannot avoid applying some theory to this type of data.

At the same time, traditional survey techniques pre-suppose that communities or individuals are capable of understanding the questions posed and of supplying pertinent replies. But, what about illiterates? And, how are those who live in very primitive and remote communities (such as women in the Brazilian hinterland) supposed to respond? What is the social authority of the researcher in such cases?

Visual evidence can have more weight than verbal enquiry in such situations. For instance, video can be a more appropriate tool for participatory research because it can record authentic lifestyles and customs. However once again, the researcher needs to constantly refer to theory and reformulate this in the light of the evidence collected. Hence, the praxis of the research is regularly reviewed.

In Social Psychology investigation, the researcher must work with conceptual references which are embedded in visual Anthropology. Elements such as body language and imagination theory come into play in an effort to explain the major differences observed between what the research subjects might say and what they actually experience. In our own investigations, we have found that it was necessary to adapt both our own praxis and the more traditional research techniques to deal with the reality of the subject under study.

Changing Ideas

The concept of sustainable development is very different from the North and South viewpoints, as the Brundtland Report clearly demonstrated when it stated:

"To satisfy necessities and human aspirations is the main objective of development. In the underdeveloped countries, the basic necessities for a great majority of people - food, clothing, housing, work - are actually being provided".[27]

One essential component is often omitted in relation to the countries of the South - namely, education. For all developing nations, whatever their particular stage in the process, this is a priority. Brazil is no exception to this rule.

Education must always seek to harmonize cultural and economic development so that people can work (and so be self-sufficient) while still maintaining their cultural origins and identity. This is the most serious challenge facing policy-makers and educators in today's world.

As we have stated, this concept is crucial to the development process. Up till now, the approach to different communities has been very sexist, and little or no consideration has been given to the special needs or conditions of women.

Brazil must initiate major changes in this domain since current vital societal processes such as legislation and social practices do not take account of the reality of women's lives. For instance, some 20% of households are now headed by women - yet they are forbidden, by law, to receive land from the state. This privilege is reserved for men. Another example is the use of sterilization which continues to be an abusive practice used on many women who arrive at fertility. In Sociology and Social Psychology, theory has been elaborated for men in the general sense of the word. These need to be adapted to reflect the very different realities of life for men and women.

Conclusion

This chapter has endeavoured to describe the justification for the teaching of Development Studies as an academic discipline and some of the problems involved in this task in the Brazilian context.

We have tried to show that profound reflection is required by the academic community so that meaningful social progress can come about. Thus, change is necessary - in the curriculum, in the field of university pedagogy and in our own responsibility to advance the development process within our own country.

The gender dimension is at the heart of this challenge because of its inextricable links with social change. This is the case not only in Brazil but for all nations.

Notes

1.   The UFRJ has some 37,000 teachers, 15,000 staff and 28,000 students. Its
      institutes, colleges and schools almost all offer undergraduate and post-
      graduate training. It has some of the major research centres in Latin
      America.

2.   The UFRJ/UNESCO Chair Programme in Sustainable Development is
      hosted by the Institute of Psychology.

3.   The CIEC-Contemporary Study Centre, founded by Professor Heloisa
      Buarque de Hollanda, is now called the Advanced Programme of
      Contemporary Studies.

4.   *Ecologia, Feminismo e Desenvolvimento* published under the EICOS
      Programme and co-ordinated by Professors D'Avilo Neto and
      Vasconcelos.

5.   "IBGE and Mujeres Latino Americanas en Cifras", CEPIA, FLACSO,
      1993, Demo, Pedro-Cidadania Menor, Ed. Vozes, 1991.

6.   Mies, M. *Women's Studies International Forum*, Vol. 13, No 5, pp 433-
      4411990.

7.   Hanmer, J. *Faire des Vagues, les Etudes Féminines et le Mouvement des
      Femmes*. Presented at the Groupe d'Epistemologie en Sciences Sociales,
      co-ordinated by Jacqueline Feldman, CNRS, Paris and involving an ad
      hoc group of the International Sociological Association (ISA).

8.   Harding, S. *The Science Question in Feminism*. Open University Press,
      1986.

9.   Fox-Keller, E. *Reflections on Gender and Science*. Yale University Press,
      1985.

10.   Merchant, C. *The Death of Nature - Women, Ecology and Scientific
      Revolution*. Harper and Row, 1980.

11.   "Divers Aspects de la Science et de la Critiques Féministes:le point de vue
      d'une androgyne pluridisciplinaire." GEMAS, CNRS, 1990.

12.   Some studies published in *Feminism and Psychology* Vol. 4, No. 4,
      November 1994, are dedicated to the debate on the inclusion of the issues
      of sexual differences in education and research.

13. Interview published in *El Pais*, September 1994

14. Shiva, V. cited by D'Avilo Neto and Vasconcelos in *Ecology, Feminism and Development*, Documenta EICOS, UFRJ, No 1, 1993.

15. Shiva, V. Op. cit.

16. Guillaumin, C. *Sexe, Race et Pratique du Pouvoir*. Editions Coté Femmes, 1992.

17. D'Avilo-Neto, M. I. "La Mission de la Co-operation Internationale au Développment: transmission ou sousmission?" Paper presented at the International Seminar on Development "Alms or Co-operation", Finland 1989

18. Collin, J. *La Participation des Femmes à la vie culturelle et artistique*. UNESCO, 1992.

19. Collin, F. in *Essentialisme et Dissymétrie des Sexes*. Cahiers du Grif, Printemps 1989.

20. These texts are found in *Philosophie de l'Amour* (Rivages 1988) *and Philosophie de la Modernité* (Payot 1983).

21. Simmel, G. Op.cit.

22. In Collin, J. Op. cit.

23. The three main areas of the Master's degree in Communities and Social Psychology are:
    • Communities, Environment and Development
    • Social Representation and Identity
    • Gender, Environment and Social Development

24. This finding links to our 1980s research on Authoritarianism and Stigma - Study of Social Prejudice in Brazil (to be completed).

25. The UNITWIN/UNESCO Chairs Programme can introduče important changes via the creation of inter-university networking and by promoting curricular innovation. The UNESCO Chair in Sustainable Development at the UFRJ (and involving the EICOS Programme) was established by an agreement signed in October 1993.

26. Apple, M. *Ideology and Curriculum*. Routledge and Kegan Paul, 1979

27. Nosso Futuro Comum (*Our Common Future*), World Commission on Environment and Development, FGV, RJ 2nd Edition, p.46, 1991.

Women's Health:
A Model of an Integrated Curriculum

Katherine Sherif, M.D. and Sandra P. Levison, M.D.
Medical College of Pennsylvania and Hahnemann University
Philadelphia, PA, USA

The authors wish to thank Amy Clouse, M.D. for her assistance in preparing this manuscript which has been supported in part by a grant from the Fund for the Improvement of Post-Secondary Education, U.S. Department of Education.

Introduction

In the United States, women represent more than one half the population and constitute more than sixty percent of health care visits. However, women have been underserved by the medical profession most likely because they have been excluded from leadership and decision-making in government, science, health care delivery and education. Therefore, because women have had little representation or voice in the medical and scientific establishments these fields have prioritized the concerns of men. This has not been a conspiracy against women on the part of male physicians and scientists, but a reflection of the cultural bias of which these men have been unaware.[1] Women have been excluded as subjects from important research studies for various reasons, as if the data collected on men was equally applicable to women. For example, the Physicians Health Study showed that taking aspirin could reduce the incidence of heart attacks in men. The study included more than twenty thousand men and no women, even though heart disease is the number one killer of women. The Baltimore Longitudinal Study of Aging, a long term study on this process, included only men during its first twenty years despite the fact that two-thirds of those over age 65 in the U.S. are women. The appetite suppressant phenylpropanolamine was tested primarily on young men, although those who use these diet aids are overwhelmingly women. The efficacy of aspirin in preventing migraine headaches was studied in men although women suffer from migraines three times more often.

There are gender differences between men and women that extend beyond reproduction, and there is growing recognition that women's health is more than just reproductive health. A more expanded view of the health care needs of women has resulted in the following definition: "Women's Health is devoted to facilitating the preservation of wellness and prevention of illness in women, and includes screening, diagnosing and managing conditions which are *unique* to women, are *more common* in women, are *more serious* in women, have manifestations, *risk factors* or *interventions* which are different for women. It also recognizes the importance of the study of gender differences, recognizes multi-disciplinary team approaches, includes the values and knowledge of women and their own experience of health and illness, recognizes the diversity of women's health needs over their life span, and how these needs reflect differences in race, class, ethnicity, culture, sexual orientation and levels of education and access to medical care, includes the empowerment of women, as for all patients, to be informed participants in their own health care."[2] In contrast to other definitions of women's health, which emphasize the absence of disease, this definition emphasizes prevention and wellness. It also acknowledges a patient physician partnership, the input of women and the need for close collaboration with allied health professionals. This definition recognizes the differences that diversity plays in women's health which are reflected in ethnicity, race, sexuality, culture and economic status. A corollary of this definition is a change in health care beneficiaries from white women to all women.

Trends and Issues related to Women's Health

In the U.S. female patients and the health care establishment are pressing to eliminate the fragmentation of health care. While many women have received total care from their obstetrician gynaecologists or family physicians, most women have received fragmented health care - being attended by two or three physicians - an internist, family physician and an obstetrician/gynaecologist.

Moreover, the move to generalism aims for "one stop shopping." This will require that internists and family practitioners become more skilled in performing office gynaecology for well women and that obstetricians and gynaecologists who aim at delivering more generalized care should become more knowledgeable about common non-reproductive health maintenance.

Pregnancy and child care

For centuries, pregnancy and child care were considered normal life phenomena. Women were tended by other women and nurse midwives. However, at the turn of this century it was recognized that many maternal deaths were due to bacterial infection and that many cases of chronic pelvic pain and infertility were caused by undiagnosed pelvic inflammatory disease. Physicians took over deliveries and gynaecological disease management as the field of obstetrics and gynaecology developed. Many aspects of the services provided by obstetrician gynaecologists were surgically based. What followed was the "medicalization" of almost every aspect of women's health from menstruation to childbirth to menopause.[3] As a result of the "medicalization" of pregnancy many of the normal aspects of pregnancy, delivery and the post-partum period were discarded.[3] Natural child birth was eliminated in Western countries and so, in the 1960s and 1970s, women had to fight to deliver a child without anaesthetic intervention.

Similarly, information about breastfeeding was not taught in medical schools during most of this century and physicians encouraged mothers not to breastfeed but to use newborn cows' milk. In the 1960s and 1970s, women faced an uphill struggle to breastfeed and had to turn to self help organizations like the La Leche League in order to be able to perform a very natural and beneficial biological function that women in more traditional societies were doing, but which was not available to middle class women in the United States because of insufficient information. An adversarial relationship developed between women who wanted to breastfeed or be assured of an anaesthetic-free delivery in order to have a healthy baby and physicians who knew nothing about either. In fact, many physicians could not understand why women wanted to suffer pain. Mothers of these women could not help them because they had no experience on which to draw. American women had to seek advice and education abroad. The publication of *Our Bodies, Ourselves* is hailed by women as a reclaiming of their participation in their health care management.[4]

Why has the medical establishment been slow to respond? Almost everyone agrees that the absence of women in positions of power, in general, and in medicine and government, left women without a voice in a variety of important forums. Rendered invisible and voiceless, women have depended on their husbands, lovers, brothers and fathers to protect them and to have their needs met. This has been very unsatisfactory. Women have become infuriated because what they assess as their medical needs have been unmet. At the same time male physicians who have been sincere, hardworking and advocates for their female patients feel betrayed by what they perceive as lack of gratitude by their demands and complaints. In addition, many women patients feel the same way about women physicians as they do with their male counterparts and have looked elsewhere to midwives, nurses and social workers, because they believe that the patriarchal medical establishment has mentored women physicians in a way that makes them non-representative of women patients. In summary, women's health care needs have been defined by the providers rather than by the women involved.

Women's needs

It is now generally agreed that women should be served better by the medical profession. That there is a real omission in teaching about women's health is also no longer debatable. In 1994, discussions in the United States Congress acknowledged the lack of provision of comprehensive primary health care for women, and expressed concern about the current inadequacy of women's health training in medical school education. It was recommended that schools of medicine and osteopathy be surveyed to determine the amount and content of academic and clinical training in women's health beyond clerkships and courses in obstetrics and gynaecology, and finally that a model of a women's health core curriculum be developed. It was also recommended that there should be improvement in competencies in training in the care of women, with the goal of educating all physicians in the full range of women's health issues and ending the fragmentation of women's health care.[5] The survey was circulated by the Association of American Medical Colleges and the results will be reported to both houses this spring.

Gender-related disorders

Disorders which occur more commonly in women than in men include depression and anxiety disorders; collagen vascular diseases such as rheumatoid arthritis, scleroderma, and systemic lupus erythematosus; breast cancer; osteoporosis; and eating disorders which are primarily found in the U.S. and Europe but are almost unheard of in the rest of the world. Examples of diseases which are unique to women are ovarian cancer, endometrial cancer, endometriosis, polycystic ovarian disease, the premenstrual syndrome/late luteal phase dysphoria and interstitial cystitis.

Gender differences occur in Physiology and Biochemistry. Women metabolize alcohol more slowly than men because of decreased alcohol dehydrogenase enzyme activity.[6] Alcohol intoxication and cirrhosis of the liver may occur at a more rapid rate in women than men. In a study of African-American women in the U.S., women showed greater insulin sensitivity than did men.[7] In addition there are racial differences in enzyme activity.

Different disease processes not only affect women differently than men, they affect subgroups of women differently. Nulliparous women and women who deliver their first child after age thirty-five are at greater risk of breast cancer, as are women whose age of onset of menstruation is earlier and who undergo menopause earlier.[8]

Subgroup vulnerability
Socio-economic status and gender roles also interact with Physiology to explain differences in mortality in subgroups. For example, African-American women die more often from breast cancer in the U.S. than other women,[9] while Latina women in the U.S. have higher morbidity and mortality from cervical cancer than other women.[10] One in three lesbians develops cancer, a higher incidence than in all women.[11] Women diagnosed with AIDS die sooner than men who present with AIDS. This may reflect gender differences in the immune response to HIV infection, lack of familiarity of health care workers with the presentation of HIV in women, or the late presentation of women with HIV because of their poor economic situation and lack of health insurance. Worldwide, malaria and schistosomiasis, the two most common parasitic diseases have a greater morbidity and mortality in women than in men.[12]

Many preventive care needs of women such as nutrition, prevention of transmission of sexually transmitted diseases (STDs) and smoking cessation differ from men. Outside the Western world, the most common complication arising from the puerperium are hemorrhage and infection, which are responsible for twenty percent of all maternal deaths.[13] Poor nutrition directly contributes to shock and death since severe chronic anaemia is ubiquitous in these women and renders them with no reserve against post-partum hemorrhage. Malnutrition also impairs the body's ability to fight infection and post-partum infection is common in these locations. The Nurses' Health Study has shown that even mild weight gain in women (as little as 10-15 pounds) is a significant cardiovascular risk factor.[14] Preventive efforts must focus on exercise for girls and women who traditionally have not been encouraged to take part in physical activity. Sedentary lives and the lack of weight-bearing exercise also contribute to osteoporosis and the risk of bone fracture. In the U.S., hip fracture in elderly women results in a 33% mortality rate within one year, a very significant factor in morbidity and cause of mortality.[15]

The smoking and the tobacco industry's efforts to target women and girls, especially in the developing world and in the minority communities of the U.S. have increased the prevalence of smoking in young women.[16] In the U.S., lung cancer has surpassed breast cancer as the leading cause of death from cancer in women, although the world statistics for their susceptibility to this disease are not yet known. Smoking is also correlated with the development of cervical cancer.

Preventive efforts are also needed to halt the transmission of the Human Immunodeficiency Virus (HIV) in women. These strategies must reflect not only biological factors but an understanding of the cultural, legal and economic conditions which influence HIV transmission. The incidence of HIV in the U.S. has been rapidly increasing, "Adolescents, women, racial/ethnic minorities, and persons infected through injecting drug use or heterosexual contact had the largest increase in case reporting."[17] Women who live in societies where there is no legal protection against domestic violence or marital rape, and who do not have the power to determine the conditions under which they will have sex will not benefit from instruction about the use of condoms or abstinence. Other STDs, such as chlamydia and gonorrhea, are a major cause of infertility.

Neglected fields of health care

Traditionally, women's health has been synonymous with reproductive health. However, many areas of "reproductive health" have been neglected, including menstruation, menopause, endometriosis, premenstrual/late-luteal phase dysphoria syndrome, infertility, lactation, breastfeeding and safe contraception. Some contraceptives and abortifacients which are safe and effective, such as the "morning-after pill," are not widely known or used, while others, such as RU-486, have not been tested in the U.S. due to political pressure on the manufacturers.

The effects of the menstrual cycle on metabolism and the pharmacokinetics of drugs is essentially unknown; for example, in some diabetic women, red blood cells bind to insulin differently during the menstrual cycle making insulin requirements vary.[18] This change in insulin dosage reflects different physiology rather than non-compliance. Estrogen and progesterone influence sphincter tone and gastric motility. Stomach emptying affects the absorption and metabolism of drugs. We need to know more about the influence of menstruation, menopause and hormone replacement therapy (HRT) on drug metabolism.

Health care issues of family planning, including pre-conceptual planning, contraception and abortion, have been so politicized that they are either omitted or inadequately addressed in the medical curriculum. Consequently, there are too few health care providers offering these services. In 1995, the American College of Graduate Medical Education (ACGME) reaffirmed the requirement for residents in Obstetrics and Gynaecology to be taught about performing abortions. The only exceptions were for those with moral or religious objections.

While medical students are repetitively taught about the examination of the lungs and heart, the pelvic and breast exam may be introduced briefly in the preclinical years and then revisited during a clerkship in Obstetrics and Gynaecology.

Ironically, the lack of detailed training of medical students and residents in breast and pelvic exams has resulted in further fragmentation of care. With the exception of some family physicians, breast surgeons and obstetrician gynaecologists, most physicians do not feel confident in their skills in this area and refer patients to "specialists."

The natural effects of aging on growth hormone levels, ovulatory cycles and other organ systems must be better taught. In addition, normal and abnormal processes should be considered over the lifespan.

Results of cosmetic treatment and other practices
Standards of beauty which vary from location and culture often impact negatively on the health of girls and women. They vary from the more benign wearing of high-heeled shoes by Western women which slows gait and shortens the gastrocnemius tendon to the binding of feet in China. Female genital mutilation (FGM) of girls, also known as female circumcision, is practiced in many different forms and cultures across the Asian and African continents. The various forms of FGM lead to loss of sexual pleasure, infection, fistulae formation, deformity, chronic pain, and death.[19] FGM cannot be addressed without an understanding of the underlying reasons for this ritual and its central importance in women's status in some cultures. In Western countries, the internalization of impossible standards of beauty has resulted in the enormous growth of the plastic surgery industry. Women seek multiple surgeries such as rhinoplasty, breast augmentation and reduction, liposuction, and "tummy tucks" in order to conform to a standard of beauty that resembles an adolescent boy's body. These women place themselves at surgical risk when they undergo elective surgery. Despite surgery these women often are dissatisfied because they expect the surgery and their appearance to improve their lives. The binding of feet and FGM are done to little girls while grown women choose plastic surgery.

Towards an understanding of women's health

The most complex issues in understanding women's health revolve around the interconnection of gender roles, social status, economic status and health. The most important issue internationally is the issue of access to health care. The barriers to receiving health care are multiple and depend on the society. The biggest barrier is poverty and lack of insurance. Women, who are often defined through their marital status, may be poor because they are unmarried or may lack insurance because their husband lacks insurance due to unemployment. In industrialized, relatively wealthy nations, there are vast populations that are underserved. In the U.S., it is postulated that poverty is responsible for the higher mortality rate seen in African-American women diagnosed with breast cancer. Lack of education is another factor in access, both on the part of women and their practitioners. Many poor and disadvantaged women lack an awareness of the importance of PAP smears in the early detection of cervical cancer and the increased risk of cervical cancer in smokers and in the sexually active who do not use barrier methods. This may lead to unnecessary morbidity and mortality.

Many physicians lack knowledge of the signs and symptoms specific for women and this may lead them to underdiagnose cardiovascular diseases and AIDS in women. In addition, male physicians are much less likely to order routine screening mammograms and Pap smears than female physicians.[20] Other obstacles to access include the politicization of and opposition to abortion and contraception, which have decreased the numbers of practitioners providing these services, decreased the number of medical schools teaching these subjects, and created a dangerous climate for those who continue to provide abortion services.[21]

In many societies, married women have higher status than unmarried women and in some cultures, mothers of boys have greater status than the mothers of girls. There are medical implications of the greater societal value of women who bear male children. In hopes of producing a son, women may have multiple pregnancies, amniocentesis or ultrasound for sex selection and abortion of female fetuses. Ultimately, a woman may be rejected by her husband and his family for failure to produce sons. Ironically, it is the fathers who contribute the Y chromosome that is the sex-determining chromosome in a fetus. Fertility is so crucial to women's social status and identity that in some parts of the Middle East, menopause is referred to as "sanat al yaas" or "the age of desperation." Childbearing is so central to some cultures that there is often tension between the need to limit family size due to poverty and the concern by certain populations that Western-financed family planning agencies are racist bodies that promote contraception to limit the number of births of babies of color. Development agencies in the past have imposed their own values on nations without an understanding of cultural values. Finally, the phenomenon of baby-selling by a poor underclass to meet the needs of the wealthy to acquire infants with "desirable" characteristics has taken an ugly twist in the U.S. with the introduction of lawyer-brokered "surrogate motherhood arrangements."[22]

While Western societies claim to value men and women equally, reports of lower rates of renal transplantation,[23] access to cardiac surgery and invasive diagnostic and therapeutic interventions[24] in women have questioned this.

Factors affecting women's health

Education
Lack of formal education for many girls and women prevents opportunities that lead to intellectual growth and self-actualization. The costs in terms of mental and spiritual health are immeasurable. Although men are also denied opportunities to learn, chiefly due to poverty and lack of education, there is a systematic bias against educating girls all over the world. The discrimination that prevents educated women from achieving professional advancement (the glass ceiling) and that isolates

women in all professions and businesses creates stress and alienation. The micro-inequities take the form of not taking women seriously, not including women in networking, not mentoring women, ignoring, interrupting, excluding, devaluing and harassing women.[25] [26] The struggle for respect and validation distracts women from achieving their goals.

Economy

The economic status of women factory workers in Asia, the latest global arena for the exploitation of cheap unskilled labour by multi-national companies, forces women to live and work under inhumane and dangerous conditions. The forces that create these conditions are multi-faceted and include the entry of multi-national companies into countries that are forced to accept the terms and conditions of the International Monetary Fund (IMF) and the World Bank (WB) in order to restructure debt. The economic policies of organizations such as the IMF and WB indirectly affect the health of millions; those health problems cannot be dealt with on a meaningful scale without addressing the problems of structural adjustment programmes imposed by these organizations. Similarly, it is not enough for the governments of some Asian countries to wage an extensive public campaign advocating condom use as a means of preventing HIV transmission without addressing the economic conditions that created the vast prostitution industry.[27] The entreaties of governments for wider condom use seem meaningless in this context, especially when women working as prostitutes are unable to use condoms and would not, even if they could, due to vaginal abrasions. "Health care" for these women and girls must be viewed in a human rights and economic context in order to influence change.

Physical abuse

Violence against women, especially by intimates, is an international health problem. For some time, violence against women has been the major cause of emergency room visits in the U.S. (one out of five visits) but is just emerging as a "health" issue[28] and the necessary interventions are still not made.[29] Physicians and health care workers have not regularly inquired about the possibility of violence even when women clearly have suspicious injuries. Until recently, the medical curriculum has not placed adequate emphasis on the detection and treatment of targets of violence. Assistance for these women has commonly been provided by non-medical community action groups. The psychological consequences of violence (including rape) also covers the post-traumatic stress disorder.[30] If untreated, these often result in the development of eating disorders and multiple somatic complaints.

Nutrition
The impact of nutrition on women's health includes an understanding of cultural norms about what foods are eaten by which people. In some cultures, the most nutritious, protein-rich foods are given to men only, resulting in systematic chronic malnutrition for women and girls. In those cultures where custom or religion dictate that men are fed first and receive larger portions of food, boys are fed next, and girls and women last, women become anaemic and less able to fight infection.

Gender roles with regards to chastity, "purity," and marriageability cause needless suffering for hundreds of thousands of women due to ritual female genital mutilation. Yet, when attempts are made to raise public awareness regarding female circumcision, these can meet with serious opposition.[31]

The Role of the Medical Curricula

The exclusion of women physicians from leadership positions in the medical establishment has excluded women from the decision-making process. Therefore, medical curricula reflect the concerns and priorities of male physicians, educators and scientists. In order for health care to be truly woman-centered, women must be part of the leadership in medical schools and the medical establishment. The following example developed by Lawrence and Weinhouse[3] describes how a health care issue like domestic violence would be approached if it were truly woman-centered:

1. Violence against girls and women would be recognized as an epidemic.
2. Medical research would devote billions of dollars to implement a cure.
3. Violence against girls and women would be recognized as a disease of men, not women.
4. Cure would be based on changing male behaviours.
5. There would be diagnostic labels in the Psychiatry Diagnostic and Statistic Manual (DSM) for this problem of male aggression.[3]
6. Insurance companies would not be permitted to penalize female targets of violence as having a "prior condition" and, therefore, render them uninsurable.

Until recently, U.S. society has condoned violence against women. Laws and the criminal justice system have not protected women against abuse, and the movies and television have depicted aggressive behaviour against women in such a glamorous and routine way that society has become numb and insensitive to brutality against girls and women. Additionally, if between twenty and thirty percent of women have been targets of violence, many physicians have personally been exposed to violence and abuse in their own families and therefore may never have dealt with their own feelings and biases. Training must now aim at education of health care professionals to recognize their personal bias so they can be better able to help their patients.

The Professional Status of Women in Medicine

The improvement in the professional status of women in medicine is inseparable from the improvement of their care. In order to improve the health care of girls and women, there must be a concerted effort by international organizations, governments, health professional schools, research institutes, accrediting bodies, professional organizations, hospitals and clinics to advance the professional development of women in health care and government leadership. Women, including those from under-represented groups, must be in leadership positions in medical research, curricular design and implementation, and health care delivery in order for the needs of women to be met. The existence of a "glass ceiling" which has prevented the promotion and retention of women into government and medical leadership requires a multi-prong approach. Institutions must recognize that their previous policies and procedures often discriminated against women. Therefore, there must be a systematic effort to create policies and educate leadership to ensure salary equity and the promotion of women, with a recognition of the differences in credentials that women may possess which reflects their disproportionate involvement in childbirth, child rearing, the care of other family members, previous discrimination and lack of merit promotion. In addition, institutions must implement sexual harassment policies in order to ensure an environment in which women can work safely. In the United States, sexual harassment is illegal and the judicial system has enforced very high penalties against institutions where a hostile environment has been created because of this offence. This standard should be adopted world-wide as well as by the United Nations where several agencies have already taken active measures to protect their staff.

Influential organizations
International agencies, such as UNESCO and WHO, should strongly endorse and publicize their commitment to the improvement in health care for women and children through advances in women's health research, medical education and medical care as well as a commitment to the study of gender differences. In the U.S., competencies in women's health have been developed by the American College of Obstetrics and Gynecology, the Federated Council of Internal Medicine and

the American Medical Women's Association. This work should be publicized, circulated and used as a template by accrediting bodies, medical schools, health professional schools, health examination boards and international organizations. In the U.S., as a result of a survey conducted by the National Institutes of Health (NIH) Office of Research on Women's Health and the Health Resources and Services Administration in collaboration with the Association of American Medical Colleges, schools of medicine and osteopathy are now re-examining their curricula to include gender differences and women's health learning. Such efforts should extend to all health care professional schools worldwide. Assessment tools must be developed in women's health.

International bodies must encourage universities and medical schools to emphasize the power of physicians and health care providers in their patient relationships. The potential for abuse in these professional relationships should be recognized and strategies to avoid and discourage such abuse should be implemented. Because of the differential of power, patients must be educated so they can better participate in their care. UNESCO should encourage co-operation between women's health caregivers and an interdisciplinary approach. Above all, turf battles must be discouraged. UNESCO and WHO should acknowledge gender bias in medical educational materials and could develop task forces to examine this material and eliminate such bias. In addition, health care providers should be educated about the prevalence of these problems in learning materials and research references.

Innovative Medical Curricula: the MCPHE Case

In 1993, with the support from a grant from the Fund for the Improvement of Post Secondary Education (FIPSE) of the U.S. Department of Education and matching college funds, the Medical College of Pennsylvania (previously named Women's Medical College and now called the Medical College of

Pennsylvania and Hahnemann University [MCPHU]) undertook a commitment to integrate women's health education into the medical school curriculum. A Women's Health Education Programme (WHEP) was created, along with the hiring of an expert in Women's Studies and gender issues, support staff and the naming of a director. The curriculum that has been developed and implemented is to serve as a template for other institutions. Curricular efforts were initiated in the first two years of medical school and then rapidly extended throughout the entire four years of the medical school curriculum, post-graduate residency training and continuing medical education and faculty development. Improving the knowledge of medical student teachers, residents and faculty is vital to curricular change. At MCPHU, women's health education is seen as the responsibility of every faculty member and women's health care the responsibility of every physician. Such policies should be adopted universally in order to improve women's health education and care.

The goals and objectives of the WHEP at MCPHU are to improve the health care of all women by developing, implementing and evaluating a curriculum that teaches medical students, post-graduate trainees, physicians and eventually all those who care for patients the knowledge, skills and attitudes required to maintain women's health through disease prevention, diagnosis and treatment.

Topics addressed by the programme include:
- differences between women and men with respect to Anatomy, Physiology, Microbiology and Biochemistry
- presentation and pathophysiology of diseases as well as pharmacology of drugs used to treat them
- diseases that are unique to or more common in women
- factors determining women's wellness over their life span
- frequency of abuse and violence against girls and women so that they can be properly diagnosed and treated

- health policies and practice changes necessary to address the needs of all women and children in the health care delivery system
- history which determined the current state of knowledge and health care delivery patterns for all women in the U.S.
- understanding of the problems and requirements of conducting research in women
- recognizing the changes in women and their health care needs over their life span.

Skills that are taught include:
- respectful treatment of women
- the establishment of adequate medical histories for women
- appropriate physical assessment which demonstrates sensitivity and knowledge important to women
- helping women to have access to care
- empowering women to participate in decision-making and disease prevention
- delivering health care as part of a multidisciplinary team.

Finally, physician attitudes and communication:
- are demonstrated by doctors themselves and so, particularly when the gender of the physician and patient are different, should ensure appropriate health care for women
- should teach an appreciation of the power of the physician
- should indicate an understanding of the diversity of women in the community based on differences in race, culture, ethnicity, sexuality, class, social and economic factors and how these impact on health care.

The following techniques have been implemented to insert meaningful women's health learning into the curricula:
- case-based learning
- Women's Health Grand Rounds
- Women's Health Colloquia and Journal Club
- standardized patients for training
- bulletin boards displaying resources on women's health

- faculty development through programmes such as ELAM (Emerging Leaders in Academic Medicine)
- role-playing
- guest lecturers
- small group sessions
- use of a guide to bias-free language
- analysis of student and physician bias
- special reference library collection.

At MCPHU, we believe that women's health care is the responsibility of every physician and that all teachers should be skilled in instruction about gender differences. This assures that women's health is taught throughout the curriculum and is not marginalized to an elective course. In addition, we support the notion that some physicians and researchers wish to intensify their knowledge of women's health and that they receive opportunities to receive special training. However, in the United States at this time, there is pressure for training in general medicine and it is unlikely that the formal accreditation of new sub-specialties will be supported.

While WHEP was analyzing the curriculum for gaps in women's health education, the MCPHU Dean and Provost created the Institute for Women's Health (IWH). The IWH consists of several divisions. It absorbed the existent Archives and Special Collections of Women in Medicine (a vast collection of books, articles, photos and memorabilia that document the contributions of women in medicine). The faculty Committee of Women in Medicine was created to address important issues which are relevant to the development and advancement of women faculty members. These issues have included the development of an institutional sexual harassment policy and a maternity leave policy. Another division was created to develop teaching programmes aimed specifically at women who wished to develop careers in academic medicine, Emerging Leaders in Academic Medicine (ELAM). The ELAM programme aims at educating faculty from all institutions. A Centre of Women's Health Care had been created several years previously to end the fragmented delivery of their treatment via an interdisciplinary approach. The general internist offers usual women's health preventive and primary care along with normal office gynaecology. An obstetrician gynaecologist is on site, as needed, along with facilities for x-ray, mammography, bone densitometry, nutrition and exercise counselling. The National Academy of Women's Health Medical Education (NAWHME) was created by MCP and the American Medical Women's Association (AMWA) to infuse women's health into the curricula of all medical schools and hospitals. An endowed chair was created in Women's Health for the Director of the Institute for Women's Health. This model of the IWH is working well at MCPHU. However, we recognize differences in other organizations, countries and medical schools and recommend that they make the particular changes appropriate for their own environment.

Conclusion

It is important to emphasize that women's health is not achieved at the expense of men. The examination of gender differences and the exploration of patient needs in their life context should improve health care for both men and women. Finally, improved health care for women also results in improved well being for children and families because of women's role in caregiving. In order to see rapid improvement in women's health and professional development, enlightened and supportive men should be actively recruited to join these efforts.

Bibliography

1.   Nechas E, Foley D. *Unequal Treatment: What You Don't Know About How Women Are Mistreated by the Medical Community.* New York, NY: Simon & Schuster; 1994.

2.   National Academy on Women's Health Medical Education (NAWHME) Medical College of Pennsylvania and Hahnemann University Broad and Vine Streets MS 490 Philadelphia, PA 19102.

3.   Lawrence L, Weinhouse B. *Outrageous Practices: The Alarming Truth About How Medicine Mistreats Women*. New York, NY: Fawcett Columbine; 1994.

4.   Boston Women's Health Collective. *Our Bodies, Ourselves*. New York, NY: Simon & Schuster; 1971.

5.   Minority Health Improvement Act of 1994. U.S. House of Representatives 3869.
     Departments of Labor, Health and Human Services, and Education and Related Agencies Appropriation Bill, 1994. U.S. House of Representatives.
     Departments of Labor, Health and Human Services, and Education and Related Agencies Appropriation Bill, 1993. U.S. Senate.

6.   Roine R. "First pass metabolism of alcohol and its significance." *Nordisk Medicin*. 1991;106:325-327.

7.   Falkner B, Hulman S, Kushner H. "Gender differences in insulin-stimulated glucose utilization among African Americans." *American Journal of Hypertension*. 1994;7:948-952.

8.   Albrektsen G, Heuch I, Tretli S, Kvale G. "Breast cancer incidence before age 55 in relation to parity and age at first and last births: A prospective study of one million Norwegian women." *Epidemiology*. 1994;5:604-611.

9.   Eley JW, Hill H, Chen V, Austin D, Wesley M, Muss H, Greenberg R, Coates R, Correa P, Redmond C, Hunter C, Herman A, Kurman R, Blacklow R, Shapiro S, Edwards B. "Racial differences in survival from breast cancer: Results of the National Cancer Institute Black/White Cancer Survival Study." *JAMA*. 1994;272:947-954.

10. Morris DL, Lusero GT, Joyce EV, Hannigan EV, Tuicker ER. "Cervical cancer, a major killer of Hispanic women: Implications for health education." *Health Education*. 1989;20:23-28.

11. Rounds, K. "Are lesbians a high-risk group for breast cancer?" *Women's Health Newsletter*. Issue 19, 1993.

12. Vlassoff C, Bonilla E. "Gender-related differences in the impact of tropical diseases on women: what do we know?" *Journal of Biosocial Science*. 1994;26:37-53.

13. Urassa E, Massawe S, Mgaya H, Lindmard G, Nystrom L. "Female mortality in reproductive ages in Dar es Salaam, Tanzania." *East African Medical Journal.* 1994;71:226-231.

14. Willet W, Manson J, Stampfer M, Colditz G, Rosner B, Speizer F, Hennekens C. "Weight, weight change, and coronary heart disease in women: Risk within the 'normal' weight range." *JAMA.* 1995;273:461-465.

15. Armstrong AL, Wallace WA. "The epidemiology of hip fractures and methods of prevention." *Acta Orthopaedica Belgica.* 1994;60 Suppl 1:85-101.

16. Warner KE, Goldenhar LM, McLaughlin CG. "Cigarette advertising and magazine coverage of the hazards of smoking. A statistical analysis." *New England Journal of Medicine.* 1992;326:305-309.

17. Recent trends in U.S. "AIDS cases reported to CDC." *CDC HIV/AIDS Prevention.* 1994;5:4.

18. Bertoli A, DePirro R, Fusco A, Greco A, Magnatta R, Lauro R. "Differences in insulin receptors between men and menstruating women and influence of sex hormones on insulin binding during the menstrual cycle." *Journal of Clinical Endocrinology and Metabolism.* 1980;50:246-250.

19. Toubia N. "Female circumcision as a public health issue." *New England Journal of Medicine.* 1994;331:712-716.

20. Lurie N, Slate J, McGovern P, Ekstrum J, Quam L, Margolis K. "Preventive care for women: Does the sex of the physician matter?" *New England Journal of Medicine.* 1993;329:478-482.

21. In 1994 in the United States, five persons who worked in abortion clinics were murdered by "Pro-Life Movement" fanatics who justified the murders as a means to stopping abortions. The fanatics continue to threaten the live of physicians and to bomb dozens of abortion clinics.

22. Corea G.(ed). *Man Made Women: How New Reproductive Technologies Affect Women.* Bloomington, IN: Indiana University Press; 1987.

23. Soucie JM, Neyland JF, McClellan W. "Race and sex differences in the identification of candidates for renal transplantation." *American Journal of Kidney Diseases.* 1992;19:414-419.

24. Tobin UN, Wasswetheil-Smoller S, Wexler JP, Steingert RM, Budner N, Lense L, Wachspress J. "Sex bias in considering coronary bypass surgery." *Annals of Internal Medicine.* 1987;107:19-25.

25. Sandler, B. "The classroom climate: A chilly one for women?" *Project on the Status and Education of Women of the Association of American Colleges.* 1982.

26. Rowe MP. "Barriers to equality: The power of subtle discrimination to maintain unequal opportunity." *Employee Responsibilities and Rights Journal.* 1990;3:153-163.

27. Human Rights Watch Women's Rights Project. *A Modern Form of Slavery: Trafficking of Burmese Women and Girls into Brothels in Thailand.* New York, NY: Human Rights Watch; 1993.

28. McLeer S, Anwar R. "The role of the emergency physician in the prevention of domestic violence." *Annals of Emergency Medicine.* 1987;16:1155-1161.

29. Warshaw C. "Domestic violence: Challenge to medical practice." *Journal of Women's Health.* 1993;2:73-80.

30. Foa EB, Riggs DS, Gershuny BS. "Arousal, numbing, and intrusion: Symptom structure of PTSD following assault." *American Journal of Psychiatry.* 1995;152:116-120.

31. el Saadawi N. *The Hidden Face of Eve: Women in the Arab World.* London, UK: Zed Press; 1980.

Gender and the Curriculum in Commerce and Management Studies

Margaret Gardner and Marnie King
Griffith University, Australia

Introduction

Traditionally, education in Commerce and Management has been regarded as gender-neutral. It is only in recent decades, following the growth of Women's Studies in the Humanities and Social Sciences, that this assumption has been challenged. The study of Commerce and Management traverses a broad range of fields which themselves draw upon a range of other disciplines including Psychology, Sociology, Economics, History and Political Science. The major fields of study include Accounting, Business Computing, Organizational Behaviour, Human Resource Management, Industrial Relations, International Business, Marketing, Public Policy and Strategic Management among others. The study of Management is comparatively recent in universities and for much of the time has been the subject of postgraduate rather than undergraduate study. At undergraduate level, accounting and economics have had a longer tradition as part of the undergraduate curriculum.

Much of the development of these areas of study has grown from the assumptions of the various underlying disciplines, and has had typically a strongly positivist or "scientific" paradigm that underpinned the assumption of gender neutrality. Moreover, both students and practitioners in these fields have been predominantly male, reinforcing a gender homogeneity in culture that was largely unnoticed.

The curriculum for Management is most often seen in the Master of Business Administration (MBA) programmes that have proliferated in a number of countries. Indeed it has been suggested that the supply of MBA programmes exceeds demand in a number of countries (O'Reilly 1994; Sinclair 1995b). Undergraduate study in Commerce or Business has also burgeoned in Australia, New Zealand, the United States and the United Kingdom. Currently in Australia students in Commerce and Management programmes in higher education comprise 21% of the total student population - only students in Humanities and Social Science programmes form a larger group (DEET 1995). Three-quarters of Commerce and Management students are in undergraduate degrees. Further the number of students in Commerce and Management programmes almost doubled between 1984 and 1994 - although in part this reflects the major increase in students in higher education in Australia generally during this period according to a 1995 report of the Department of Education, Employment and Training (DEET).

Given the large proportion of students in higher education in Commerce and Management programs in Australia and many other countries, and the significance attached to management education in assisting economic growth, it is important to gauge the role of gender in the curriculum and the study of these areas.

Still (1993b) suggests gender cultures still persist in organizations and business schools. These persisting cultures are confirmed by the low representation of women in both Economics and Management programmes and in the upper echelons of the general workforce. To combat such problems Sinclair (1995b) suggests that curricula should become gender inclusive to include the experiences of women and avoid bias in the use of research, teaching methods, language use, classroom interactions and assessment methods.

The Context

Low Representation of Women in Commerce and Management Programmes

Moses (1990), in her study of Australian postgraduate students, found Economics was the most male dominated field in terms of its structures and culture. Women made up only 35% of undergraduates in Economics courses. At the Honours level, women were between 20%-25% of the students. At the higher degree level, women comprised less than 25% of the total number of students. She also found there was an extremely low proportion of female postgraduate students at the 'pure' end of the Economics programmes. One explanation for the small number of postgraduate students in Economics was excellent employment prospects for students who completed an undergraduate degree. This, however, does not explain the small number of female students who initially enrol in the undergraduate programme. Similarly, Sinclair (1995a) argues that women have been a minority group in Management education, only beginning to be admitted to MBA programmes in the 1960s and 1970s.

Table 1 indicates that overall in Australia the proportion of women in Commerce and Management programmes in universities is better than that evident in particular sub-groups such as Economics or Business Computing. At undergraduate level the proportion of women in Commerce and Management is approaching 50%, although this must be put in the context that overall women represent 55% of the undergraduate university population in Australia. The under representation of women is most marked at PhD level, which at 29% is considerably lower than the 39% of women overall in PhD programmes.

Table 1
Proportion of Females in Commerce and Management Programmes in Australian Universities, 1994

	PhD	Masters	Bachelor (Honours)	Bachelor
Females %	29.0	30.7	39.6	46.2

Source: DEET(1995a)

Moses (1990) provides various explanations based on interviews for the small numbers of women postgraduate students in Honours, Masters and PhD. These include a lack of encouragement from the faculty and academics, and a lack of visible role models in the department and profession. While numbers of women PhDs remain low, the proportion of academics who are women tends to be correspondingly low.

Lack of Role Models in Commerce and Management
There is a clear lack of female role models in Australian academia. In 1987 only 26% of Australia's academics and 3.7% of professors were women. By 1994 32.8% of Australian academics were female and 11.6% were in professorial[1] positions (DEET 1995b). Allen (1990) found that women's participation in academia was increasing slower than that of other professions such as architects, engineers, doctors, dentists, lawyers and teachers.

In the Australian workforce, women make up approximately 25.4% of all management positions (Australian Bureau of Statistics, 1994) and only 3% of Senior Executive positions (Korn/Ferry International, 1993). Two studies by Still (1993a) of women managers in the top "1000" Australian companies reveal that women were 2.5% of senior managers in 1984 and only 1.3% in 1992 and indeed the representation of women had declined in all but supervisory positions over this period.

In general, despite the comparatively high and increasing representation of women in Commerce and Management undergraduate programmes in Australia, women have very low representation in management positions, including senior positions in the public sector (around 14%) and in professions such as Accounting. It appears, therefore, that in Commerce and Management spheres, few female role models exist within academia or the workforce as a whole.

Equity Issues
It is not surprising in the context outlined above that studies examining the approach of academics to teaching in these areas find deficiencies in their appreciation of gender issues. Lewis, Davidson, French, and Sargent (1994) found in an examination of teachers as practitioners in a university School of Management that teachers were not well informed about equity policy or committed to its implementation, despite stating they agreed in principle regarding these issues. Similarly, Smith and Hutchinson (1994:2) found in the development of an MBA unit "Effective Organizations: Gender Issues in Management" that there was a "reluctance and lack of preparedness on the part of both academics and industry management to deal with these issues".

Stromquist (1993) contends that curricula have only included women's issues in feminist courses rather than integrating women's issues in all courses including Business, Economics and Management - arguing that issues of gender have been ghettoized. Examining economics textbooks in the United States, Feiner (1993) finds that authors of major introductory texts still present issues of gender (and race) in stereotypical manner. This study followed one conducted in 1987 that found gender was mentioned in less than one percent of the pages in introductory texts (Feiner and Morgan cited in Gray 1992). While specialist texts, such as Labour Economics textbooks, make more mention of gender it is nevertheless a neglected issue (Gray 1992). Sinclair (1995b) also notes that

Management theory and texts give very little discussion to women researchers, although Mary Parker Follett is one of the major early writers on Management, and Joan Woodward also had a substantial impact on the development of the field.

In Australia, Still (1993b) argues that although "Women in Management" is a theoretical and empirical field in its own right, the topic has failed to infiltrate mainstream Management theory, and remains "marginalized and segregated, similarly to the subjects it espouses to liberate" (Still, 1993b:1). Table 2 indicates those universities[2] in Australia with subjects which specifically identify women in Management or Economics. This understates the extent of gender content within broadly named subjects, but does give an indication of where the need to address gender issues is regarded as important enough to warrant specific mention. Less than half of those in the selection had subjects which indicated specifically that they dealt with gender issues, and typically this was in subjects that could be chosen as electives rather than the compulsory core of an undergraduate or postgraduate programme. There is no evidence that gender perspectives have been included in subjects such as Accounting, Finance, Information Systems and Marketing for example. In other words most of the areas that are regarded as central to programmes in Commerce and Management, with the exception of areas such as Labour Economics, Human Resource Management, Industrial Relations or General Management have apparently ignored gender issues.

Table 2 **Incidence of Subjects on Women in Commerce and Management in Australian Universities** is on the following pages.

University	Year	Women in Manage-ment or Economics Specifically Men-tioned in Subject Titles/Descriptions	Subject Title And Description
Australian Catholic University, Queensland, Faculty of Arts and Science.	1994	NO	-
Bond University, School of Business.	1994	NO	-
Charles Sturt University, Faculty of Commerce, undergraduate and postgraduate.	1995	NO	-
Curtin University, Business School.	1995	NO	-
Deakin University, Undergraduate Studies, Faculty of Management.	1995	NO	-
Edith Cowan University, Faculty of Business.	1996	YES	*Effective Organisations: Gender Issues In Management.*
Flinders University, Faculty of Social Sciences.	1995	NO	-
Griffith University Faculty of Commerce and Administration, and Graduate School of Management.	1995	YES	*Foundations of Commerce and Administration; Labour Economic Issues; Industrial Relations Policies* in the Bachelor of Commerce. *Gender, Ethnicity and Work; Equal Employment Opportunity Practice and Law* electives in Master of Business Administration and Master of Public Sector Management

University	Year	Women in Management......	Subject Title And Description
James Cook University, Faculty of Commerce and Economics.	1995	YES	*Graduate Diploma of Women's Studies.* The subject considers the impact of gender on leadership styles and management techniques used in business organizations.
Macquarie University, School of Economic and Financial Studies.	1995	YES	*Labour Market Policies* in the School of Economic and Financial Studies. Changes in the labour force affecting the age, sex and occupational composition of the workforce. Segmentation and discrimination in labour markets.
Murdoch University, School of Economics.	1995	NO	-
Northern Territory University, Faculty of Business.	1995	NO	-
QUT, Faculty of Business.	1995	YES	*Equity at Work*, in Management Major Options.
RMIT , Undergraduate and Postgraduate, Department of Economics and Finance and Department of Management.	1995	YES	*Sex, Gender and Society* offered in the Context Curriculum Unit.

University	Year	Women In Management...	Subject Title And Description
The University of Southern Queensland, Faculty of Business.	1995	NO	-
The University of Sydney, Department of Economic History and Department of Economics.	1992	YES	*Early Economic History* ...Such themes as the role of women... *Economics IIP (1)(2)* ...the framework involves the dynamic interactions between capital, labour, the family and the state, the sexual division of labour... *Political Economy of Women* (Option).
University of Central Queensland, Faculty of Business.	1995	NO	-
University of Newcastle, Faculty of Economics and Commerce.	1994	NO	-
University of South Australia, Faculty of Business Management.	1994	YES	*Women and Economics* (Economics Option in the Bachelor of Applied Economics).
University of Tasmania, Faculty of Commerce and Economics.	1995	NO	-
University of Western Sydney, Macarthur, Faculty of Commerce and Economics and Faculty of Business and Technology.	1995	NO	-
Hawkesbury, Faculty of Management.	1994	NO	-

While women are today an increasing proportion of the students and the practitioners of commerce and management in Australia, they have for some time had very limited representation. Women remain clearly in the minority among academics, particularly senior academics, and senior managers. They have in consequence limited visibility and impact on the curriculum. The curriculum lags considerably behind broad changes occurring in the participation of women in work and in universities in societies such as Australia. In general, the major texts in commerce and management, and the undergraduate and postgraduate curriculum presume gender neutrality while demonstrating gender blindness.

Towards Gender Inclusiveness

Gender Inclusiveness and Mainstreaming Gender Issues
The need to mainstream gender issues in the university curriculum is legitimate given that women represent over 50% of humanity. Kearney (1995) suggests that an example of this in the Commerce and Management spheres is taking account of the role of women in the economic development of a given society within the curriculum. Furthermore, the *Global Framework for the Draft Platform for Action* suggests that to address women's access to quality education and training for self-reliance at all levels and in all fields and sectors, education should be made gender sensitive. They suggest that this may be achieved by eliminating social stereotypes from curricula, and encouraging textbooks, teacher training and materials which represent women positively. Furthermore, they suggest that research perpetrated by women about women should be encouraged in all spheres. The Commerce and Management area is critical - but, as yet, has given little attention to the curriculum and the way that university teaching may disseminate models of appropriate management

styles and policies that do not reflect adequately women's experience.

Gender Inclusiveness and Management Curriculum

Sinclair (1995b) believes that female experience must be integrated into the curriculum to attain a gender inclusive curriculum. She contends that women have been disadvantaged in the curriculum for Management education as this has been based on male experiences, consumers and careers. She defines "gender-inclusive curriculum" as recognizing the "knowledge and experience of women as being just as valid and relevant as the knowledge and experience of men in mainstream academic discourse". The application of "gender inclusiveness" to curriculum includes addressing issues such as how, and how well, Management is taught and including the experiences of women. It includes avoiding bias in teaching methods, language use, class interactions and assessment methods.

Sinclair favours the gender inclusive approach to "gender blindness" which makes no reference to gender. She believes that it is dangerous and ineffective to be "gender blind" as the dominant male paradigm remains as an unchallenged and accepted norm. Essentially, women remain invisible in the curriculum. Sinclair illustrates the exclusionary nature of "gender blindness". For example, theories which have evolved from studies containing all male participants and authors may contain an inherent gender bias. Ignoring gender as a factor allows any bias to remain unexamined. Much Management education encourages particular styles of leadership which may exclude many women (Still 1993b, Sinclair 1994, Bellamy et al 1994). Often the solution proffered to deal with the small proportion of women in these leadership roles involves emulating male models. An example of such a solution is postulated by Marshall (1984) who calls for training, career development and mentoring relationships to increase women's prospects in management jobs. She believes that this is achieved, however, by training women to participate in employment in similar ways to men. Gender inclusiveness strives to acknowledge the experiences of both women and men and refutes the assumption that the male experience is the definitive norm, by changing the way all management subjects are delivered.

More commonly, redressing the gender imbalance in the curriculum has been dealt with by the development of specific subjects. Unfortunately, as noted above, these subjects are usually elective or optional. Smith and Hutchinson (1994) describe the development of such a specific subject on "Effective Organizations: Gender Issues in Management", but propose this as a core subject within Management studies.

This unit is divided into three modules which examine the external environment, the gendered nature of organizational culture and strategies for change. It looks at women's participation in the political, industrial and socio-economic spheres, recognizing informal and formal structures and men and women within these areas.

> It examines the way in which leadership and management styles interact with the position, power and contribution of women in organizations, and contribute to gender stereotyping. The gendered nature of the organization culture, structures and processes, and their effect on the effective participation of women in management, are explored in detail. Strategies for recognizing, utilizing and maximizing the contribution of women in management levels of organizations are identified. (Smith and Hutchinson 1994:8).

Gender Inclusive Teaching and Learning
Sullivan and Buttner (1992) contend that gender inclusive teaching and learning goes beyond curriculum content and gender issues and that differences in the classroom should be

recognized and addressed. They note that instructors "focus eye contact on men, allow interruptions of women's comments, rephrase women's comments give greater public praise to men and ask women 'lower-order' factual questions" (Sullivan and Buttner 1992:81). Moses (1990) found that women were less likely than men to continue into postgraduate education due to lack of encouragement.

Sinclair (1995b) suggests that teachers become aware of cues which may alert them to women being excluded from teaching. She also suggests avoiding men's and women's stereotypes when providing teaching examples. Lewis et al (1994) found that academics in their university were taking steps to include women in the Management curriculum. For example, they had changed overheads, unit outlines, pointed out discriminatory language, used gender-inclusive language in teaching, corrected students who used "male" terminology and outlined non-discriminatory presentation and practice policy in week one of each semester. Smith and Hutchinson (1994) in developing a curriculum unit within an MBA, sought to develop content, structure, presentation and delivery which challenged traditional management education theory and practice. They also allowed for the use of flexible delivery styles in the unit, such as distance education and university based intensive study to make the subject more accessible to women.

Conclusion

Australia suffers low representation of women in Commerce and Management areas of academia and the upper echelons of the workforce. To combat such problems it has been suggested to remove "gender blindness" from the curriculum so that biases against women are revealed and removed. Gender blindness should be replaced with "gender-inclusiveness". This involves a major re-examination of curriculum in all Management subjects, not just the development of subjects that deal with gender issues. It also means critical reflection on the styles of teaching and learning used in Commerce and Management so that the involvement of women is encouraged and diversity of experience recognized. There are examples of such developments in some universities, but they remain unusual. There needs to be encouragement of development of curriculum materials that will enable more staff teaching in commerce and management areas to reflect the growing diversity of the student body and the workforce.

Notes

1. This is not a direct comparison with the earlier cited statistic since it includes associate professors and professors. The academic hierarchy in Australia has associate lecturers or tutors at the bottom, and in ascending order lecturers, senior lecturers (the career grade), associate professors and professors. Overall professorial staff are less than 20% of all academic staff.

2. This list does not include all Australian universities (which total around 36) but a broad and representative selection.

Bibliography

Draft Platform for Action. Draft document for the 4th World Conference on Women, United Nations, 1994

Affirmative Action Agency. *Affirmative Action: Guidelines for Implementation in Institutions of Higher Education.* Canberra: Australian Government Publishing Service, 1987.

Affirmative Action Agency. *By Steps and Degrees: Affirmative action initiatives from higher education institutions.* Canberra: Australian Government Publishing Service, 1992.

Affirmative Action Agency. *Introduction to Affirmative Action: Guidelines for Developing and Implementing an Affirmative Action Program.* Canberra: Australian Government Publishing Service, 1993.

Allen, F. *Academic Women in Australian Universities*. Canberra: Australian Government Printing Service, 1990.

Bellamy, P. and K. Ramsay *Barriers to Women Working in Corporate Management,* Canberra: Australian Government Publishing Service, 1994.

Catanese, A. "Faculty Role Models and Diversifying the Gender and Racial Mix of Undergraduate Economics Majors." *Journal of Economic Education,* 22(3):276-284,1991.

Davis, E., M., Pratt, V., (Eds) *Making the Link: affirmative action and industrial relations*. Canberra: Affirmative Action Agency, Labour Market Studies Foundation, 1990.

DEET. (Department of Education, Employment and Training). *Selected Higher Education Student Statistics 1994,* Canberra: Australian Government Publishing Service, 1995a.

DEET. *Selected Higher Education Staff Statistics 1994* Canberra: Australian Government Publishing Service, 1995b.

Feiner, S. Introductory Economics Textbooks and the Treatment of Issues Relating to Women and Minorities 1984 and 1991, *Journal of Economic Education,* 24(2):145-162, 1993.

Gray, T. Women in Labor Economics Textbooks, *Journal of Economic Education,* 23(4):362-373.

Harman, K. 1991 Book Review: Moses, I., 1990 Barriers to Women's Participation as Postgraduate Students in *Journal of Tertiary Education Administration,* 13(2):190-191, 1992.

Jin, P. and Low, R. *The Tao of* Management, 1991*: The Dialectical Yin-Yang Model and its Challenge to Current Management Practice.* Paper Presented at the ANZAME Conference, 1994.

Kearney, M. *Women and the University Curriculum: Towards Equality, Democracy and Peace*: Position Paper for the IFUW Triennial Conference. UNESCO, 1995.

Korn/Ferry International in conjunction with Australian Institute of Company Directors. *Twelfth study of boards of directors in Australia*. Sydney: Korn/Ferry International, 1993.

Lewis, D., Davidson, P., French, E., Sargent, L. *Managing Equity in a School of Management: Academics Self-Examine.* Paper Presented at the ANZAM Conference 1994.

Marshall, J. *Women Managers: Travellers in a Male World.* Brisbane: John Wiley & Sons, 1984.

Moses, I. *Barriers to Women's Participation as Postgraduate Students.* Canberra: R.D. Rubie, Commonwealth Government Printer, 1990.

Sinclair, A. *Trials at the Top: Chief Executives Talk about Men, Women and Australian Executive Culture,* Melbourne: The Australian Centre, 1994.

Sinclair, A. *The MBA Through Women's Eyes: Learning and Pedagogy in Management Education.* (unpublished paper), 1995a.

Sinclair, A. (forthcoming) *Gender in the Management Curricula.* Melbourne: Equal Opportunity Office, The University of Melbourne, 1995b.

Smith, C. R. and. Hutchinson, J. *Addressing Gender Issues in Management Education: The Imperative for Enhancing Australian Organisational Effectiveness.* Paper Presented at the Australia and New Zealand Academy of Management ANZAM) Conference, 1994.

Still, L.V. *Where To From Here? The Managerial Woman in Transition* , Sydney: Business and Professional Publishing, 1993a.

Still, L.V. *Women in Management: The forgotten theory in practice, or how not to change a culture. Women in Management Series*, Paper No. 18, School of Business, University of Western Sydney, Nepean, New South Wales, 1993b.

Stromquist, N. P. "Sex-Equity Legislation in Education: The State as Promoter of Women's Rights." *Review of Educational Research*, 63(4) p379-407, 1993.

Sullivan, S. and Buttner, E. "Changing More than the Plumbing: Integrating Women and Gender Differences into Management and Organisational Behaviour Courses." *Journal of Management Education* 16(1):76-81, 1992.

Note

Legislative background

Stromquist (1993) argues that legislation allows for sex equity in education. She suggests that legislation is the precursor of the distribution of resources which in turn transforms educational organisations, students' education aspirations and improves women's educational conditions.

Higher Education in Australia is influenced by at least two Acts, the *Sex Discrimination Act 1984* and the *Affirmative Action Equal Employment Opportunity for Women) Act 1986*. The *Sex Discrimination Act 1984* "outlaws discrimination against people based on the grounds of **sex**, marital status or pregnancy in the areas of work, accommodation, **education**, the provision of goods, facilities and services, the disposal of land, the activities of clubs and the administration of Commonwealth laws and programs"Davis and Pratt, 1991:79). Whilst the *Affirmative Action Equal Employment Opportunity for Women) Act 1986* "covers private sector employees with 100 or more employees and **higher education institutions**. Employers covered in the Act are required to take eight specific steps aimed to remove discrimination towards women and promote equality in employment for women...Affirmative action programs are a planned approach to **identifying and removing structural barriers which prevent or inhibit women from fully participating in the workforce**" Davis and Pratt, 1991:79). The penalty for not complying with this Act is for the company to be mentioned in Federal Parliament.

The Curriculum in the Humanities:
A Case Study and some Reflections

Anne Holden Rønning
University of Bergen, Norway

Introduction

The Humanities is a text-based discipline where knowledge of the world is mediated through language, and where gender can be used as a lens to view the text (Schmitz 1985). Study within the Humanities is related to questions of value, interpretation being a key word in the methodology. In this lies an inherent danger, as has been seen in several countries, of indoctrination through a rewriting and reinterpretation of the historical basis of the culture. Women are often written out within the Humanities. The past experience of both genders should form the basis of present action and interpretation, and this requires a holistic gender perspective. This chapter will assess the state of the curriculum in the Humanities in Norway, and internationally. As one of the oldest academic fields, the dominant ideology of the curriculum in the Humanities in Europe is historically based on an elitist patriarchal and historical tradition, as underlined by the etymological derivation of the word. It may be said to represent "high" as opposed to "low" culture. This model of elitist tradition has been transmitted through colonization to most parts of the world. Recent trends have, however, seen an increasing Americanization of the system. I shall base my comments on key criteria for curriculum evaluation: **who** is being taught and the different levels of study; the **methodology** of teaching; the **context** and **content** of subjects within the Humanities; and the **incorporation** of the gender dimension within the subject, and look at these in the Norwegian context.

133

The situation in Norway

Norway has four universities Oslo (1811), Bergen (1946), Trondheim (1971) Tromsø (1972) as well as several regional colleges which give courses corresponding to the lower levels of university study. All these educational institutions are state funded, and have similar systems, governed by politically determined rules. In fact, the power of the Ministry of Education, Research and Church Affairs through its control over funding is a powerful element in determining what students may study and where.

An attempt has been made to create a Norwegian-network within different fields in order to concentrate specialization in one place. This has not been too successful, especially in the Humanities, as each university wants to be able to offer the maximum range of subjects to its students. The examination system still dominates with the consequent result this has on the curriculum.

Norway (pop. 4.3 mill.) has a high percentage of female university students. Women account for 56% of all new students, and 54% of the total number of students at universities and colleges of higher education (1993 figures) though it should be noted that only 43% of the graduates at higher levels are women, as opposed to 61% at the first degree level. In languages they make up 72% of the total. Although admission to some courses in the Humanities is selective, lectures are open. Examinations are open to all registered students whether they attend courses or not.

Despite a preferential programme for promoting qualified women, the latest statistics show that the number of women professors is well under 10%, and there are many departments and research institutes, even in the humanities, which have no women professors. The situation is, however, better in the humanities than in other fields, for example, at the Norwegian Advanced College of Technology female professors account for 0.7% of the total, and at the Norwegian College of Economics and Business Administration there are no female professors at all. The percentage of women staff in the Humanities is, however, fairly high in relation to the university as a whole. Until recently (1994) the University of Bergen has practised positive discrimination for appointments with the aim of ensuring that 40% of the staff within each faculty shall be of the "under-represented" gender. This policy has worked to some extent, but has had some strange results, as it works by faculty not by department. This has resulted in some subject areas having a dominance of women, as in my own department, English, which has at present a ratio of 11 women to 5 men on the permanent staff. It is interesting to note that all the men are full professors, but only one of the women holds this rank. Other departments such as History and Philosophy, Classics and Norwegian either have no women at all, or have their token woman, one or two at the most. The impact of this on the gender-specificity of different subject areas is obvious. It is unfortunate that the inclusion of a gender perspective is so dependent on the number of female staff, though some few men are exceptions to the rule.

Methodology
Methodology covers the criteria we use in selection and evaluation of a curriculum and the methods used to transmit subject knowledge. Selection criteria are often based on comparative length and content, but Norway also has a system of granting time for time, i.e. one year's study anywhere else can count as one year's study in the subject area at lower levels, providing the size of the syllabus is relatively the same. This is a quantitative rather than qualitative norm. While the structure of the curriculum is approved quantitatively by the university administration, the content is up to the individual department and often the individual interests of the members of staff. The dominant teaching methodology is lecturing especially at the lower levels, with seminars and group work at higher levels. This

allows for considerable freedom for the promotion of the individual's own gender-specific views, whether positive or negative. Pedagogical qualifications have until very recently not been requirements for university professors and teachers. This can be seen as inhibiting to new and constructive ways of introducing a gender-perspective here. The methodological basis now demanded at school level has not yet filtered through into higher education.

Context and content

At the University of Bergen, the Humanities covers a wider field than in some other countries, and comprises foreign languages (with an emphasis on literature and linguistics), Comparative Literature, Norwegian, Phonetics and Linguistics, Philosophy, History, Archaeology and Museums, Theatre Science, History of Art, Ethnology, Classics and History of Religions. There are Centres for European Cultural Studies, for the Study of the Sciences and the Humanities, and for Feminist Research in the Humanities The last-mentioned is a permanent institution, focusing on disseminating feminist research, but has suffered from a lack of adequate funding or staffing. None of these centres have the right to give courses or examinations which give credits, in contrast to similar institutions at some other Norwegian universities which are often more interdisciplinary The content of the Humanities is roughly the same throughout Norway, though in some universities such as Tromsø, History is in the Social Sciences Faculty.

The course system is relatively alike all over Norway, and degrees are standardized. Students take a four-year first degree (cand. mag.) consisting of a half-year preliminary course in Philosophy followed by three subjects, studied at two levels. Each student must take a major subject at both levels. This may be followed by a two-year Master's course in the subject one has majored in. It is perhaps interesting to note that the Norwegian Research Council Evaluation of English Studies in Norway in 1991 found "that both the curricula and the teaching structure in

English ... too conventional." The same would apply to most subjects within the Humanities.

Space does not allow me to give a detailed survey of all fields in this paper so I shall concentrate my comments on four main areas, Literature, Linguistics, History and Philosophy.

Literature

The content and context of literature vary according to language, but the general approach is a historically and theoretically based model of study. In foreign languages, literature is usually seen as a social and cultural artefact in society, a study of which can provide the student not only with theoretical models, but also insight into the social forces out of which the literature sprung. The gender dimension is considered important for a total view of the society in which we live. We do not consider the inclusion of women's texts and gender-specific areas of study as sufficient, but also concentrate on the gender perspective in texts by men.

Literature and cultural studies (institutions and the history of ideas) are closely linked in all study of foreign languages in Norway. Recent trends are to advertise positions jointly in civilization and literature, a positive trend in terms of gender studies, as literature may be used to exemplify, even if fictional, the realities of social norms and political processes. Areas of special research and value for establishing an understanding of development, equality and peace which have been taught in my department are courses at both higher and lower levels in both major and minor programmes, in post-colonial studies and Afro-American studies with their theoretical basis in concepts such as "cultural identity" "national identity", and "hybridity". There has been a marked increase in interest in these areas within Norway as a whole. Cultural studies is an area where gender analysis is particularly important, but course content tends to be fairly traditional. The inclusion of gender is often limited to discussing political leaders like Margaret Thatcher, the women's emancipation movement, women's autobiography or topics such as advertising and ideology. These courses, however, are primarily given by female members of staff.

Courses in women's literature have been given since 1976, also by men. Feminist theoretical positions, both European and Anglo-American, and feminist texts are taught in several departments, and feminist theories may be said to have played a key role in much recent research undertaken in the Humanities. The Norwegian Research Council had a five-year programme from 1989-1994 where scholarships for established scholars as well as doctoral students were made available for work within Women's Studies, a follow-up of a programme in literature started in the late 1970s.

Departments of Norwegian play an important role in preserving, disseminating and publicising aspects of Norwegian language, culture and literature, but it seems the gender perspective has mainly been dependent on there being female members of staff who are interested. This varies according to university, and Tromsø could be cited as an example of how a gender perspective may be incorporated into all branches of literature. The organisation of all languages and literature into a joint Institute for Language and Literature at the University of Tromsø, has had positive results in opening up for a broader gender perspective.

An example of feminist Nordic co-operation in the field of literature and cultural studies is the publication of a pioneer work *Kvinnenes Kulturhistorie* (Women's Cultural History) in three volumes (1985-88), a world history of women and their culture researched and edited by women.

Linguistics

Norway has a very active linguistic environment, which includes Computational Linguistics. The science of written and spoken communicative skills, in the mother tongue or foreign languages, is a subject area with far-reaching consequences in society. Major areas of study in Norway are Grammar, History of Language, Sociolinguistics, Pragmatics and Applied Linguistics. Sociolinguistics is important as it opens up not just for theoretical understanding of linguistic processes, but is closely linked to cultural differences between language users. Research in Bergen and Tromsø on the study of gender differences in language, and women's language in particular, has not been sufficiently implemented. We often teach cultural differences between types of language, but this should also include more about gender differences in speech. Two projects which can be of international interest are being undertaken in Bergen, the COLT project, a study and analysis of a corpus of London teenager language, and EVA, an evaluation of the English of pupils in the secondary school (in Norway children learn English from the age of nine). In the first instance, the gender perspective has not been included, but as the gender of the recorded pupils has been noted, it is hoped the second phase of the project will include a gender component. Several linguistic projects based in Bergen are undertaken in co-operation with other universities inside and outside Norway. Computational Linguistics and Artificial Intelligence are other fields where there has been a concentration of research in Bergen.

History

Bergen had the first chair of Women's History in Norway, but we cannot say that this has resulted in the inclusion of a gender dimension throughout the courses in history. However, this professor has led some pioneering work in her field including editing the acclaimed *Cappelens Kvinnehistorie* (3 vols.) (1992-

3), a Nordic co-publication of women's history in a world perspective. History has been a male bastion, (Bergen has only 2 women on a staff of 26), and this may be said to be reflected in the lack of gender perspective in the curriculum. Courses with a conscious gender dimension are largely left to the women, and tend to focus on welfare, households and work hierarchies. A recent university course which was made for television did not have one single section on women's history in Norway.

An interesting case study has been done in Bergen of the portrayal (and absence) of women in museum exhibitions. As museums retain and transmit culture, the gender perspective is important for visualizing women in all roles, not just in the domestic sphere. The first women's museum in Norway was opened this year (1995).

Philosophy
Women philosophers are few and far between in Norway. The Department of Philosophy in Bergen has only one woman on the permanent staff and all the gender-specific courses at intermediate level are her responsibility. Courses include gender thought in the History of Philosophy, Feminist Ethics, and Feminist Philosophy. The content of the obligatory course in Philosophy, with 450 pages, has only 75 which relate to women. In more recent thinking, only Mary Wollstonecraft and Simone de Beauvoir are included.

It is obvious that, though on paper universities such as Bergen have a high percentage of courses which offer a gender dimension in the curriculum, the dependency of these courses on individual scholars makes them highly vulnerable to extinction, and many students may pass through the system without being offered courses with any specific gender perspective. This is a fairly common situation all over Europe, and seemingly an international trend. If we are to have a genuine gender balance in the curriculum, it is vital to break this gender/person configuration.

Gender Questions Relevant to the Humanities

The integration of feminist and gender perspectives in research at all levels may be said to be fairly well established practice in most countries. However, although the establishment of Centres for Women's Studies and Research, and Women's Studies Programmes is invaluable in the effort to get acknowledgement of the gender perspective, there is an inherent danger of these becoming female ghettos, and the authorities feeling that they have satisfied the demands for gender research simply by funding such centres.

The concept of gender dimension

A valid change in the university curriculum presupposes an adequate investigation of the concept of gender-dimension as woman is not just one construct, either. The cultural reproduction of gender is often related to class and race, as either culturally defined sexual identity, or a social construct. As a social construct it differs from culture to culture, and at different historical periods. We also have to ask questions such as whether adding a gender dimension is a pedagogical problem within the discipline, or is better solved by forming separate programmes to counteract a broader pattern of female subordination. It is not enough just to add some texts by women, or by people of varied cultural origins since the author's gender may have little bearing on a gender-specific view, and other criteria may be paramount. Another question we can ask is whether gender-stereotyping is fixed prior to coming to the university. What, then, is the university's role?

International gender questions within the Humanities

Much work has been done on curriculum transformation in America (some 200 publications in the period 1975-1992), and some exciting experiments have been carried out on innovative ways of teaching and including gender. Many of these have their basis in the gender integration model (McIntosh, 1983; Schuster & Van Dyne, 1985; Tetrault, 1980, 1985) which seeks to reform the curriculum by looking at cultural, political and social perspectives of texts such as those of the great thinkers of the past. This shows how research in a particular field has been biased. The results should be implemented internationally, as it is a process whereby the need for a gender dimension is observed, then written into the curriculum. It reveals what has been missing and questions the effect of this omission. Finally there is a concentration on the study of gender, and a reconstruction of the curriculum. Today we can say that various subject areas are at different stages along this path. It is, however, unfortunate that these projects are often linked to Women's Studies and Ethnic Studies. If we are really to transform the curriculum so as to include a world-wide gender perspective then we have to relate these methods to all subjects.

Texts, the basis of study in Humaniora, affirm the continuity and cultural distinctiveness of a society. The availability of texts, for example, in many parts of former Eastern Europe, and in parts of the Third World limit what is taught and the perspectives presented. The curriculum cannot be defined by short-term goals but should widen and expand the students' horizon to see their responsibility to the social process in which they are participating, and to work towards peace, development and equality. Unless students are enabled to comprehend the links between subject knowledge per se, and the complexity of the global society in which they live, and its effects on women in particular, benefits will not accrue to society as a whole. This should have relevance for the criteria for selection of texts, as texts form the basis of the curriculum in the Humanities. The big publishing monopolies have considerable economic and political power over what is taught, especially in the widespread use of anthologies of literature. In other words, the European elitist tradition of the Humanities is supported by capitalist forces which control what is published and by whom.

We should warn against the curriculum being too concerned with present day issues - an historical perspective is becoming increasingly important in contemporary society, when the media underscores that what happens today is the only thing of importance. For example, a reading of feminist women's texts from the 17th century can be an awakening to a student who thinks these feminist views belong only to the twentieth century. It also puts the whole perspective of the feminist claim to equality in another light. It is one way of putting such issues on the map.

The **empowerment** of women is another aspect of gender which the Humanities can contribute to by putting women's history firmly on the curriculum map, thus providing role models for change and leadership. We need a curriculum for globalization and internationalization as an antidote to the nationalistic and ethno-centric nature of history, for example. Much writing by women from former colonies and from people of other cultures, aims precisely at exposing the degradation which women have suffered, and specifically offers alternative lifestyles. This literature thus provides role models for change. Women's texts are empowering from a female viewpoint, and explanatory for a male viewpoint, but some male texts may also be empowering when read in the light of feminist criticism or in the light of historical phenomena of the day, e.g. the women's emancipation movement in different countries visible in texts.

Training is necessary in gender analysis, i.e. in seeing the gender specific nature of texts from as objective a view as possible. One of the dangers of contemporary theory, also feminist, is that it can easily become a straightjacket into which to press the text regardless of its cultural context.

Literature is a valuable tool in the search for an explanation of concepts such as displacement and alienation which have a clear gender dimension. Together with marginalization, they are good starting points for a global discussion of cultural difference, and of women's role in the world and in their own societies.

An inclusion of gender language studies as an essential part of a university curriculum in Linguistics, whether in the native tongue or foreign languages, could be a useful tool on the path towards peace and equality. For example, a study of the language of violence could show how certain words, combined with body language, bring forth violent reactions. Communication is dependent not just on the content of the words used, but on the context and the manner in which the words are used, especially when spoken. A mutual understanding of these features of language is important for both men and women, and will lead to improved communicative skills and empower women to take on leadership roles.

International communication is dependent on foreign languages and an understanding of their cultural implications, including gender aspects, is a prerequisite for development and understanding between nations. The study of linguistic models of communication between peoples of different nations and age groups, and the gender content in these, is certainly vital. Furthermore, the dissemination of this research is even more crucial.

Philosophy is important as it teaches the art of thinking i.e. logic, rhetoric, problem-solving, hypothesis testing and so forth. Philosophy, in particular, has as its fundamental basis the learning of critical evaluation of philosophical theories of values. The European tradition, which is the basis for most courses in the Humanities world-wide, has always fostered a belief in the need for a basic core curriculum in Philosophy and/or Metaphysics as a basis for any study of the Humanities. This tradition is in danger of being lost, and has already been so in some countries, and yet it is a pre-requisite for an understanding of our European cultural heritage which has a far-reaching influence on all other university systems. What is needed is a new look at the teaching of Philosophy with the inclusion of many texts by great women thinkers from antiquity up to the present.

Other gender issues could be a study of women as peacemakers, through the contrastive study of Literature and History written about war by men and women, revealing their differing experiences. This would bring out the role of the pacifists, for example.

At the local level, considerable research is being done in many countries on women in minority groups, but this needs co-ordinating and disseminating. The role of language as expressive of these groups is an area which can only adequately be dealt with at the local level. For reasons such as these, men should be encouraged to participate in programmes and research related to Women's Studies.

Strategies for establishing a dialogue with national decision-makers

The aim of UNESCO's action strategy for women in higher education is "to define and foster a gender-inclusive culture through education - and notably higher education - so as to promote sustainable human development." To achieve this goal within the Humanities, the curriculum is one of the areas where international co-operation and institutional policy-making is not only desirable, but is becoming increasingly necessary due to student mobility. There is also a need for some kind of evaluation of the context and content of the university curriculum in the Humanities at institutional level.

As receivers of university education, students are people who may later sit in positions which give them a certain power in society, whether in politics, business, or in the classroom, to influence the next generation of young people. In the Humanities, in particular, the content and context of the curricula have, therefore, far-reaching consequences outside the academic institutions where the students acquire the knowledge and skills they will later utilize. If we are to achieve a change in attitudes which will lead to peace, development and equality, we must instil in the student, through the curriculum content, an understanding of these as concepts which pervade all aspects of their work. Students must be taught to think deeply, logically and effectively.

Advocacy
Universities should utilize curriculum research and theory in the planning of new curricula. There is a need for more research into university curricula and the criteria for selection of content. Much excellent work has been done on the school curricula, but far less on the university curriculum as a whole. Looking at individual subjects, while useful in itself, fails to give the overview necessary for the student and the outside world. Comparative case studies of one individual subject in each major discipline on a world-wide basis could form the start of a programme to relate the university curriculum to the needs of society and the individual. The time has passed when subject expertise alone is the sole criteria for a syllabus.

The curriculum must be a result of conscious planning and less "unplanned" drift. As UNESCO has pointed out: "Gender impact assessment should be a mandatory process in all educational policy-making and planning." (UN report from Vienna NGO Forum 94 - Call to Action from the Economic Commission for Europe, 20 Dec. 1994 to UN Economic and Social Council). We can ask whether universities should have complete freedom in curriculum planning, or whether norms should be established for looking at the curriculum in academe in relation to the social context of higher education i.e. the cultural, political, economic and organizational influences. To avoid yet further bureaucratization of educational systems in many countries like Norway which have state education, these curriculum criteria should be an internationally recognized framework into which university curricula can fit. Curriculum standards or norms which will make it easier for degrees and academic qualifications to be recognized in other countries should be designed and implemented thereby safeguarding human rights especially those of groups such as "migrant wives" and refugees. These are the groups particularly vulnerable to mobility, and those which have most trouble having their qualifications approved. With general increased student mobility, this issue is rapidly becoming not just one for women but also for men.

Training
Students must be trained to challenge dominant values in society. This is part of the democratic process and must include attitudes towards women. If we view education as a dynamic process and people as active agents in that process, then they must be taught to think in terms of a wider perspective where the gender-dimension is included. But we must not lose sight of the overall ends of education.

A radical revision is needed of the method of teaching in the Humanities, as well as a demand for pedagogical qualifications from all academic staff, including further education from time to time in new methodologies of selection, systematization and evaluation of curricula. This is the only way to keep apace with contemporary trends in society, and provide concentration on those aspects of teaching which lead to the addition of a gender dimension, and to training in leadership skills. Leadership skills are best acquired by the student in participatory roles in the teaching situation. University teaching staff, at whatever level, provide role models not just in the theoretical method of approaching the subject under study, but in the way of presenting knowledge and communicating with other people who do not necessarily have the same expertise. Why, even today in the 1990s, is a higher university degree a key to a lecturing position and yet not to teaching in schools? This creates an artificial divide that the 18 year-old in school must have a pedagogically qualified teacher whereas the 19 year-old does not need someone with a knowledge of pedagogy. Also important in the academic community is accessibility of technological equipment and keeping up with technological advances, e.g. multi-media programmes instead of lectures, and a general move towards seminars, tutorials, and group work. This is not just a question of attitudes, but even more of funding. The Humanities are at a clear disadvantage here, as in contrast to subjects requiring laboratory space it is more difficult to find criteria other than student:staff ratio when demanding funding. Mass higher education which we are witnessing today leads to a watering down of the curriculum, and fragmentation of subject areas, unless funding is available to maintain the quality of teaching given in previous decades. A conflict can easily arise between expertise and egalitarianism.

Research

One of the major problems within academe is the "ivory tower complex". Many other subject areas have an advantage over the Humanities here, as either practical experience has been gained outside the university, or research programmes are financed and funded from external sources so there is more contact with the "real" world. Research councils which control funding have considerable power. For example, in Norway, the Humanities no longer exists as a separate funding area, but comes under the heading of "Culture and Society" - together with the Social Sciences. When applicability of research to society's needs is one of the funding criteria it is clear that the Humanities can have difficulty in proving that areas other than those of proven national interest (e.g. History and mother tongue) are priority areas.

Research is needed into the theory of curriculum, concerned with the fundamental determinants of the curriculum - its sources, composition, construction, and classification of subject areas within any given field. Topics underpinning the dynamic between higher education, women and development should also be areas of priority.

Today there is an international tendency to push the thresholds of research further and further up the scale, especially in the industrialized world. The "publish or perish" syndrome is not necessarily conducive to more valid research being done, especially in the Humanities. It has negative effects on the curriculum, as research tends to become an end in itself, rather than a basis for teaching. It is also often gender prohibitive as more women drop out, since this pressure often occurs at a time of life when women are in a reproductive phase.

Conclusion: Strategies for Action

Industry and government should be lobbied to create an understanding of the value of leadership training through the learning of independent thought processes, regardless of subject area. This should increase the leadership potential of women. A heightened awareness of the value of a degree in the Humanities is one step on the path to increased women's participation at leadership level.

Information exchange between universities as to curriculum content and context is vital if monitoring of the gender dimension is to be possible.
Universities, at regional and international level could have common norms to approve courses, and could institutionalize certain basic criteria that can be implemented for degree

equivalence. This could include assessment and evaluation of teaching processes and some kind of monitoring of exam levels. Negative systems such as the ranking of universities (e.g. in the United Kingdom) are far from ideal as they lead to a concentration of expertise - in itself, a benefit for society, but negative for the individual as this practice can cause ghettos of elitism.

Bibliography

Adams, Maurianne. ed. "Promoting Diversity in College Classrooms: Innovative Responses for the Curriculum, Faculty, and Institutions" in *New Directions for Teaching and Learning*, no. 52.

Draft Platform for Action. Draft document for the 4th World Conference on Women, United Nations, San Francisco: Jossey-Bass,1994.

UN Report to UN Economic and Social Council from Vienna NGO Forum 94 – Call to Action from the Economic Commission for Europe, 29 Dec, 1994.

Hedley, Carolyn et al. eds. *Cognition, Curriculum and Literacy*. Norwood, New Jersey; Alex Publishing Corporation, 1990.

Kelly, A.V. ed. *Curriculum Context*. London: Harper & Row, 1980.

Minifacts on Equal Status. Gender Equality Council, Norway, 1995.

Riddell, Sheila. *Gender and the Politics of the Curriculum*. London and New York: Routledge, 1992.

Schmitz, Betty, et al. *Women's Studies and Curriculum Transformation*, 1993 (forthcoming).

There are also several articles on the curriculum in *Women's Studies Quarterly*.

Women's Studies in Bulgarian Universities:
A Success Story?

Ralitsa Muharska
St Kliment Ohridski University of Sofia, Bulgaria

Introduction

This chapter discusses the problems of setting up Women's Studies as a university discipline in Bulgaria. In the context of the socio-political situation in the country and the present state of the women's movement a needs analysis is attempted. A look at the higher education situation includes the issues of access for women, and the market demand for specialists. When choosing the strategy for designing courses in Women's Studies the problematical acceptance of a feminist identity by Bulgarian women is seen as an important factor, as the cultural status of feminism is regarded as something foreign, a Western import, and therefore a vehicle of influence and domination. The viability of separating feminist theory from women's issues in general, as well as from the practice of the women's movement, for the purposes of cultural adaptation, is discussed.

Different strategies for experimenting with course content and approach are considered: introducing the basic notions of feminist theory through foreign language teaching, grouping feminist theory with other courses for cultural studies, and the possibility of giving a feminist bias to other courses regularly offered in the Humanities.

In 1991, a group of women academics from Sofia University, led by their newly acquired optimism for social change, started work on the setting up of Women's Studies as a university discipline. Like many other people in the country, we thought that the time had come for our society to shed all the trappings of the former regime. Another newly acquired incitement was the reassuring, though still scanty, knowledge about feminism, which we had been able to pick up quickly, with a lot of avid reading, after censorship was lifted in 1989.

Now, four years later having tried different strategies with little success, we are still at the phase of asking questions. This chapter is therefore concerned with formulating problems rather than with offering solutions.

There have been institutional difficulties - we assumed that institutionalization was the main problem, and started by concentrating all our efforts on attempts to get around the university's structural rigidity, its "old" (i.e. inherited), as well as "new" (i.e. recently adopted) conservatism with regard to programme innovations. These were more or less overcome as we obtained a grant and founded an independent Women's Information and Training Centre. But then we had to face the fact that in our society a growing awareness of the necessity for Women's Studies, (including feminism and a women's movement which might be led by women themselves) had been largely a product of our own wishful thinking. It became clear that a certain basic sensitivity to gender-related problems in a given society is vital if a sufficient number of people are to have the political motivation and background knowledge to become interested in the field.

A major hindrance to sensitization and consciousness-raising is the absence of any way of talking about issues of gender. The notion certainly does not exist - or translate - in our language, neither do most of the elegant terms like "gynocriticism" or "herstory", that make feminist discourse self-sufficient. In short, feminism does not "speak" Bulgarian.

The few people who are informed about - and are interested in - feminism are mainly found among those who have, in one way or another, had contact with Western European (and especially Anglo-American) culture.

So, an indispensable step in educating women about gender issues and creating a gender sensitivity in Bulgaria seems to be the building of a bridge between the languages feminism does speak - notably English - and our own language. This is a huge task as it implies the construction of an entire discourse. In a language structurally hostile, and with rigid and pervasive marking for grammatical gender that facilitates sexist usage, numerous cultural and linguistic voids need to be filled. Moreover, all this must be achieved despite the absence of a corresponding social practice. This problem requires special - and specific - attention, and so transcends the scope of the present paper.

Our task, then, needed to be approached from another angle. The same group started looking for opportunities to initiate the launching of a large-scale publicity campaign. Given our less than modest capacities and resources this was definitely a mistake, which became clear in the process. But though the scope of the task and the amount of work needed have often seemed discouraging, and despite the innumerable, often completely unexpected additional problems encountered *en route*, these efforts are continuing.

Among the numerous paradoxes and discrepancies which Bulgarian society inherited from its political past was the conviction that women have gained some equality from this system - at least on paper. This view is still generally held. This officially supported equality has to a considerable extent been responsible for preventing any real gender awareness from developing in our society. As a result, even today many members and activists in women's organizations somewhat paradoxically declare they are not feminists, often without even having a clear idea what feminism really is.

On the other hand, a strong interest in "Western" achievements in the wider sphere of social practices has produced a category of women who are aware of the positive influence of feminism and of the women's movement on social development in Europe and America during the last thirty years. So identification with feminism can be said to range all the way from unequivocal acceptance, (a small group of people), to complete denial.

The Academic Background for Women's Studies in Bulgaria

In Bulgaria there is a serious competence gap between research on women, (which quite a few academics still understand mainly as anything written about women), and teaching Women's Studies, which should, apart from discussing women's issues, presumably present feminist theory and/or practice from a consistently feminist perspective. While women as a topic are not absent from the sphere of the Social Sciences, in its assumptions, theory and methodology, this research is often at odds with feminism. On the other hand, feminism is - sporadically - present as a topic of academic or public discussion, but not as an approach. And while feminism is sometimes discussed as a school, (for example, in literary theory or cultural studies), and though its equality with other schools is taken for granted, there is a significant difference in attitude. Feminism, though deemed important, is seen as a political and tendentious fashion, and as something not very scholarly and rather transitory. There are quite a few respected scholars, who would say that "feminism is not serious". In fact, a number of people would simply refuse to discuss it - on the grounds that it "blends theory with indoctrination" and gives priority to a political perspective which is often leftist. With our heritage we in Eastern Europe have to be extremely cautious about anything ideological.

Attitudes are very similar outside academic circles - the average person has heard enough about inequality and exploitation. Such concepts have been compromised by the discrepancy between words and deeds in the past. Something new, which is modern, Western and acceptable, is met with conservatism rather than anything else. Rising nationalistic tendencies should also be noted here - since nationalism combines so easily with intolerance of all kinds. An interesting paradox about this conservatism, however, is that it is popular, though almost nobody in the country has been rich enough long enough to form its social foundation. Proclaiming themselves right-wing does not stop the majority of people from expecting the state to take care of them. In this recent confusion of right and left, maybe the kind of feminism we need to suit our amazingly contradictory society is a sort of oxymoron - namely, right-wing feminism? Living with contradiction as one does, one is tempted to wonder if such a thing would be possible. Also, our version of feminism would have to be wildly eclectic - and perhaps - completely original. What a challenge for people theoretically both innocent and "corrupt", like us, East European academics. It would also take quite some time to show results. So right now, all we can do for the purposes of teaching is just borrow ideas from diverse sources - which is a much less exciting option.

The East European Feminist Identity

In Bulgaria we have no means of defining ourselves as feminists. This is probably the case elsewhere in Eastern Europe as well. From our perspective - that of outsiders to the feminist discourse - there are many feminisms. There is the Western master-discourse, and there is us, devoid of any discourse, mute and marginal. We have no identity in feminist terms. The only way to acquire such identity seems to be by accepting some Western model and learning to "speak as feminists", to become intelligible in the already existing feminist discourse. We have to push our way into the international feminist community, which we see as an establishment, and to meet and cope with resistance and competition. In addition, once accepted, we generally seem to have a secondary status. We are required to accept certain basic conditions:

- to adopt the feminist identity as it is defined by our "other" - the West;
- to relinquish or, at least, tone down whatever other political identities we had before. This is important for people, especially in the 30-50 age group (which is usually the most active in the Western feminist movement) who have to struggle to come to terms with their East European political heritage in personal terms;
- to possess some access to the Western feminist discourse - or, to put it bluntly, to speak a West European language, preferably English. The terminology associated with gender is already undergoing some intriguing translation adventures in Eastern Europe, mostly indicating the processes and difficulties that characterize the way languages resist the acceptance of something both linguistically and culturally foreign.

Not all of us are willing to enter feminism on the West's terms - but we are still a long way from inventing our own. And although I believe that Eastern Europe has the potential - especially in terms of a specific experience - to counterbalance the domination of the Western feminist discourse with some development of its own, this process may be hindered by our impatience. The need to take a short cut and make maximum use of what is already there and ready to hand may lead us along a path that may be more complex, and consequently longer.

So, at present, inventing our own discourse is out of the question. We have no tools for this and, most importantly as I have already emphasized, intellectual effort is hardly likely to be backed up by the social practice of a politically significant women's movement.

Therefore, it looks as if the East European desire for a feminist identity may yield to the temptation to copy other efforts and so deprive itself of the possibility of choosing its path. In so doing, it may accidentally erase an interesting "otherness" and a diversity, which could benefit the global feminist community.

Who Wants Feminism in Bulgaria?

The few Bulgarian feminists, who are English-speaking, or at least have had some contact with the West, have generally learned through books what feminism has helped women achieve. They are, more often than not, insiders to the international feminist discourse, but outsiders to Bulgarian women since they have no common feminist language with them. This includes women who belong to some group, and also those who want nothing to do with organizations of any sort, and who think "dividing according to sex is just another division line in our dangerously divided society". I first heard this remark from an Estonian woman, but I have later heard the same idea repeated quite often in Bulgaria.

Do Women Want Feminism?

This question could be illustrated with numerous facts, and I feel it necessary to offer three examples which point to the same strong trend in current opinion. It seems important to do this, as it shows the difficulties we have in trying to reach a suitable audience for courses in Women's Studies.

- In December 1994, a seminar entitled "Gender Sensitization" took place at Sofia on the initiative of the Bulgarian Association of University Women (BAUW). The 40 participants were women activists from 6 East European countries, 2 West European countries and the USA. These included about 30 Bulgarians, representing small women's groups, larger women's organizations directly affiliated to political parties, as well as others with less overt connections, a couple of high profit-making women's magazines, one or two professional women's groups and a few independent individual activists. The seminar's ambitious aim - to train the participants as prospective group leaders, who would then carry out seminars of this type themselves and thus increase gender sensitivity in their respective societies - did not succeed. With two exceptions, all the Bulgarians proved to be totally unaware of even the basic concepts of feminism, such as gender and empowerment. Communicating these notions to them (by the three Western "facilitators") was difficult and lengthy. The problem was, however, not linguistic, as everyone spoke English. By the time the seminar had laboured its way through a few really key ideas, it had to end. However, at least the participants showed some genuine, if modest, curiosity about the notions that were being discussed.

- In May 1994, the American University in Bulgaria hosted a conference on mutual perspectives of women from Eastern and Western Europe. The Bulgarian participants included several women academics and about 20 representatives from a variety of women's organizations. Western participation was almost exclusively American, mostly academic. While the Bulgarian academic feminists found a lot of mutual understanding among their American counterparts, their communication with their own countrywomen, both during the discussions and in the lobbies, was a complete failure. It was so marked that it gave the conference an embarrassingly tense atmosphere. The Bulgarian feminists were regarded as people who had deliberately adopted a foreign identity to escape from their own. This was regarded as a kind of foolish snobbery and an act of blind imitation of the newly-acquired American mentor.

- A small opinion poll was carried out by the BAUW early in 1995 amongst 23 women who were asked to give their opinions anonymously. All are university lecturers from 5 state universities in 5 Bulgarian cities. Their fields cover the Humanities, Foreign Languages, Literature, Cultural Studies, Political Science and Economics. All were between 28 and 45 (with only 4 over 40), speak at least one foreign language, and all have been abroad at least once.

Almost the same number of women from very similar backgrounds were the founders of the BAUW in 1990. More importantly, they represent that limited social environment where feminism is most likely to appear in our country. The Association was going through a recruitment crisis so this opinion poll was improvised as an attempt to get at least some hints as to the possible reasons. Though women's activism is a topic for a proper sociological study, the answers do point to certain tendencies. Moreover, they coincide with what one does hear, all too often, from many educated women in Bulgaria - including women politicians, as well as members and activists of women's organizations, in the media or on public occasions.

The survey results show that:
- 5 refused to discuss feminism, saying it was nonsense (they returned the question sheets blank);
- 4 of 18 respondents said they thought of themselves as feminists, 10 said they did not, 3 gave ambiguous answers, and 1 was rather aggressively anti-feminist, and considered the movement ridiculous;
- 1 was a member of a women's organization;
- 3 would not mind joining a professional-type organization;
- 13 said they would not join and gave their reasons. Amongst the most typical were: "too busy"; "I see no reason / feel no need"; "I do not know an organization that I find attractive; "I have never been approached by one"; "I do not believe anything can be done"; "I support evolution, not revolution" (this answer, along with some others, hints at an image of feminist extremism that is strangely persistent in a society which has never witnessed anything of the sort); "there is too much opportunism behind these organizations in Bulgaria"; "any such structures are a good excuse for centralization, and therefore authoritarianism";

- 1 knew something about the women's movement in Bulgaria; 13 declared they had no idea at all whether such a thing existed.

The particular distrust of the women's movement can be illustrated by some answers to the question **What do you think of the women's movement in Bulgaria?**: "much talking, no work done"; "fortunately, not strong"; "activists pursue their own goals"; "I am against extremism"; "economic problems are more important"; "officially approved organizations that provide comfortable jobs for women with a taste for the good life" (it is true that there is one such organisation and it can unfortunately afford a lot of publicity); "too much form, too little content" and "highly official, very pompous, not effective" (the last two opinions refer to the same organization).

This sample contains, rather typically, a number of clichés that characterize public opinion about the women's movement - which itself seems to have little relation to feminism. Organizations are not trusted or are seen as ineffectual. Equality is something women in Bulgaria already have, so this is not an issue. Activists pursue their own personal advancement and nobody else's. Nothing can really be done, so why bother? To sum up, the idea of power and its distribution in the public sphere (where organizations and "structures" ought to function) is compromised in itself, which makes it extremely difficult to focus on the empowerment of women, even in a presumably tolerant - and even friendly - social context.

Such attitudes reflect the retreat from political activity in Bulgaria - a trend which in my opinion is visible elsewhere in Eastern Europe. Disappointment is making people - and women especially - return to the private sphere. Too many think the effort put into changing society between 1990 - 1993 was wasted. The young are politically apathetic - many are aware that the country's political orientation is mainly determined by the votes of senior citizens (i.e. pensioners who, at the moment, number almost as many as the active work force). Students cannot be expected to choose a course out of political motivation, and indeed it is very probable that they would avoid one with such a bias.

On the other hand, the national authorities, faced with many serious social problems, are all too happy if some of these can be addressed by the population itself, in an organized form or not, and on a voluntary basis that requires no funding. One would expect that this would result in an upsurge of activities at grass-roots level. Unfortunately, this is not the case. Besides, there is a continuing lack of communication between the few women's organizations there are and the authorities at all levels. Each side regards the other as a giver, not a receiver, of help. In the context of my analysis, this means that authorities, especially on the local, level are not to be relied on as potential employers of Women's Studies graduates. Since the state is unable to fund the kind of social work that ought to help improve the condition of women, this does not enhance the justification of the status of Women's Studies as an academic discipline. There is no market demand for such specialists. In other words, they have hardly any chance of being state-employed.

The Situation of Bulgarian Higher Education

In general, interest in higher education reflects the professional labour market in the country at the present time, and is very unevenly distributed. It is modest in the humanities, even less in the Sciences, and disproportionately strong in Law and Economics, which indicates a strong pragmatic tendency. When choosing their courses, students now tend to go for practical skills, rather than mind-broadening theory. As they are aware that the state will hardly be in a position to finance research for quite some time to come, very few people want to study, say, Physics. There is no doubt that those who have so far profited from restitution and privatization are lawyers, plus of course, the new class of businessmen.

Private initiatives in education are gaining momentum, particularly in higher learning, which both follows and reinforces this pragmatic trend.

It should also be noted that higher education in Bulgaria is, at the moment, "lawless". The old centralized way of management through the Ministry of Education has to some extent been disrupted by the autonomy of individual institutions. So far, this has been vaguely proclaimed as a general principle, rather than anything else. However, the legislation necessary to really put this principle into practice has not yet reached the top of the parliamentary agenda. This affects the launching of any innovative strategy in education.

Women in Higher Education

Women's access to higher education, while limited in fields that give training for professions deemed to be dangerous or otherwise unsuitable, is also indirectly limited in all fields by special quotas for men. These are of two kinds: for men who apply immediately after leaving secondary school, and for those who apply after they have completed their 18 -months compulsory military service. These quotas enable boys, who generally do not do as well as girls in the admission tests, to become students by competing among themselves. Girls generally do better although the admission tests are extremely stressful and student-unfriendly, requiring a lot of memorization and strict adherence to standard essay formats. They do not really give a clear picture of the applicants' critical abilities, but rather of how much they "know".

The diminishing possibilities for lifelong education should perhaps be mentioned here, as these have provided important educational opportunities for women with families.

Teaching Women's Studies

I have tried to give a more or less objective picture of the women's movement and its standing in Bulgaria, -though I am aware that my own disappointment at the present state of affairs is probably clear. What I see as pre-requisites for the academic development of Women's Studies is the socio-political background of the women's movement, plus the theory and ideology of feminism. There is an intimate connection between the history and experience of women's political activities and the perspective offered by feminist theory for interpreting this history. Furthermore, the ideological light shed upon individual women's everyday experience comes from a mixed knowledge of these two factors. In other words, by teaching women to understand what has been and is happening to them as a group, and providing a feminist interpretation of the facts, they can be trained as feminist scholars - imbued with feminist ideology, which, for its part, derives its credibility from the presence of these facts in a given society. The women's movement gave rise to feminist ideology, while feminism itself is the pillar that supports the women's movement.

Students of Women's Studies can acquire knowledge of the empowerment process. Women's studies can also be incorporated into the women's movement, to work for women and increase the social space occupied by women, sometimes in a direct and practical way. The sense of receiving a cultural heritage and an awareness of the fact that considerable achievements have been made to date are important factors in both academic and feminist motivation. However, these factors do not seem to work outside the specific, and particularly Anglo-American, cultural context. It is difficult to be inspired by a foreign heritage, so the lack of cultural motivation needs to be supplemented by something else - perhaps by a stronger feminist and political motivation. Yet, as I already pointed out, it is precisely the lack of this type of consciousness that poses the most serious problem.

Basing Women's Studies on social practice is impossible and irrelevant in Bulgaria for a number of reasons. The basic ones amongst these are:

- gender-specific sociological information is insufficient and scattered; there are vast blank areas (e. g. domestic violence, girls' socialization);
- the women's movement, apart from not being a particularly well researched area, remains associated with the former political regime. The negative image of the woman activist has not disappeared as a number of the former "women's nomenclatura" are still in force. On the other hand, in Bulgaria, we can hardly say that the movement ever achieved anything. Nor was it even moderately influential or active on the political stage. In fact, it was hardly worthy of its name.

We also have to face the problem of feminism's "foreigness". It would be pointless to attempt to answer the question whether it can be "adopted", "imitated" or "followed". The next question that arises, then, is whether a course in Women's Studies should be grouped amongst other courses related to cultural studies? Should it be approached as something culture-specific? In practical terms, the easiest way out - and the one most likely to be chosen at Sofia University - is to incorporate it into American Studies or European Studies, though neither is a degree programme on its own yet. This could prove to be an academically successful strategy. But it would keep Women's Studies in the sphere of culture-specific (and probably also theory-oriented) academic subjects. This will certainly fail to boost motivation. By remaining purely academic, Women's Studies cannot hope to be politically important, and the question of empowerment could simply be forgotten, particularly with regard to short term goals. Empowerment comes when one has internalized the ideology. But, in the interests of attracting students, we need to downplay the ideology - and notably the political and consciousness-raising aspects.

In addition, the negative images of feminism prevalent in our society must be handled in a very cautious manner, as this could emphasize the foreigness of Women's Studies still further and could work against the idea of the integration of Bulgarian women into the Western and global feminist movement. Feminism then would be seen as a kind of cultural practice among other cultural practices, distant, and not particularly appealing. It would be seen as the history of a social movement that passed us by, and of achievements - and sometimes problems -that are not ours. Consequently, it would seem a path that is too well-trodden to be challenging.

On the other hand, it is tempting to follow the already familiar tendency of demanding from the West what has been "kept from us" for so long, of borrowing ready-made models to save effort and "compensate" for the missed decades of social evolution. Any summary of the history of the women's movement in the West would inevitably reveal patterns that are tempting to follow. This also emphasizes our position of otherness, marginality and passivity with respect to what - from our perspective - is the Western feminist establishment. But at this point in time, the number of people who believe in borrowing ready-made models seems to be diminishing, and so such an approach would hardly be popular.

As a possible alternative, we are considering introducing feminist theory first. This means separating feminist theory from feminist socio-political practice. But this is artificial, and thus leads to a paradox: if one does not know about the political practice of feminism and has no consciousness of the power relations involved, one is not motivated to study the theory based on that practice. Theory is the least culture-specific part of feminism. Hence, one could argue that it is necessary to teach theory first in order to understand its potential for altering the patriarchal nature of social structures. The theory thus aims at the core of patriarchal power, rather than at various short-term goals, important as these may be. If this path is taken, the stress should fall on the really far-reaching influence of feminist theory, even if its effects will be slow in coming in comparison with some political achievements of the Western women's movement. These potential effects, though less immediate, appear to deserve very serious attention.

Moreover, I find it logical that East European feminist discourse and theory should develop before East European feminist political practice. This is realistic since the women's movement in Eastern Europe is still in a very preliminary phase, and likely to stay so for quite some time. Our attempts at feminist research and even at theory, though not numerous, seem rather impressive in comparison.

However, the question remains, who is actually interested in theory?

If it is taught separately, it would be hard to predict the outcome since theory and practice are usually considered together. Also, a separate approach implies that Women's Studies, as a discipline, has every chance of staying marginal. It would most likely become an elective course or perhaps, with luck, a minor programme in the curriculum. So this academic marginality, added to the other inherent marginalities (i.e. cultural and political specificity, or, alternatively, purely theoretical abstraction) may also impede its acceptance and normalization in Bulgarian higher education.

Another possibility is the introduction of a feminist perspective in other disciplines - for example, in the Humanities. This has already been done by a number of teachers, especially in the field of literature. This is difficult to do in an unobtrusive and natural way in courses that are taught in Bulgarian. For technical reasons, it would take considerable time to introduce the necessary discourse. However, this strategy could be useful in terms of creating an initial awareness of feminist issues and, at least, an initial cultural readiness to discuss them. Such a discussion would require a considerable degree of cultural broadmindedness and tolerance, which, it should be admitted, is something our society is still acquiring. So, we must be patient and opt for small but achievable goals. At the same time, we must continue to ask why our society, having accepted so many Western things in such an amazingly short time, has been so consistently reluctant in matters related to women?

An alternative strategy that we tried at Sofia University - with partial success - was attacking the language barrier. All graduate programmes at Sofia University include 60 hours of specific purposes oriented foreign language. We designed a course entitled "English for Feminists" for graduate students which aimed at improving foreign language communication skills, starting at Intermediate to Higher Intermediate level. At the same time students become familiar with some basic notions and terminology of feminist theory and practice. With some valuable support from the BBC ELT section, such as recordings of thematically suitable texts, the course was launched in 1993 and was quite successful for an experimental programme with an enrolment of 10. The next year, however, only 5 people applied, so it was not repeated. The reason seemed to be that enrolment was sought from a very small student contingent - female graduate students from the Humanities with a relatively high level of foreign language proficiency.

Conclusion: Towards Empowerment?

Admittedly the situation outlined above does not give much ground for optimism in terms of immediate results. The rapid and direct empowerment of women is not likely to be expected as an outcome. The slow laborious phase of gradually arousing interest cannot, as we had enthusiastically hoped, be avoided. Empowerment is a consequence of established traditions of successful feminist claims to power. The fact that Women's Studies is actually taught at many universities is part of that empowerment.

In trying to reverse the natural historical logic of this process, we in Bulgaria have been struggling with additional difficulties. The marginality of Women's Studies in the academic programme plus the marginality of women's issues in Bulgaria work together against empowerment, rather than for it. Nevertheless, our efforts are continuing.

We will be successful if we can, at this stage, help increase the number of women in our society who are individually empowered by a heightened awareness of both the facts of feminist achievements and those related to women's underprivileged position in society.

Science and Technology in China: Successes and Challenges for Women's Participation

Zhizhen Gui
(**Hong Wang** collaborated in the preparation of this chapter)
China College for Women Administrators, People's Republic of China

Introduction

Women make up half of the world's population and thus deserve to share fully in the planning and implementation of development policies. This is especially important in the fields of Science and Technology which contribute so significantly to the level of economic progress of each nation. Thus, the participation of women in this field may be considered as a key indicator with regard to their equal access to and involvement in the entire process of social development.

Women, Science and Technology - the Current Situation in China

The Early Context
An analysis of social development in China must commence far back in time when the country was run as a feudal system. This was an unhappy time for women who often experienced oppression, debasement and exclusion from all walks of life.

Above all, women were expected to obey and to submit to male authority in their families - to fathers, husbands and sons. Independence was virtually impossible, and even those few who dared to seek some measure of freedom usually met with failure, and even with disaster. This was typical of life in old China where the economy was underdeveloped. It was also true of scientific and technological advancement. In such a society, women had no part to play in social or economic progress.

Towards Change

Major changes started to occur after the founding of the People's Republic of China. The national economy underwent massive restructuring, and the national priority was development. It was essential to invest in Science and Technology so that domains such as industry and agriculture could rapidly evolve and flourish. Human resource training was also essential in these fields in order to lead the way towards modernization.

Government policy was to attract nationals with expertise, but working abroad to return home. In this way, they could contribute to the economic transformation of the country. For example, a 1956 survey showed that nearly two thousand specialists and scholars had returned from Europe, the United States, and Japan. This group included the first generation of Chinese women scientists. In 1980, the Academy of China had 15 women members, of whom 11 had returned from abroad. These included 6 physicists and 5 chemists, 3 of them the country's leading scientists - He Huizhe, the first women nuclear physicist, Lin Lanying, an expert in semi-conductor materials and Ye Shuihua, an astronomist, and the first women to head an observatory in China.

In the new China, the government attached great importance to the development of higher education. This included the training of scientists and technicians in adequate numbers and the inclusion of women in these areas. In just ten short years, there was a four-fold increase in the number of higher education institutions while overall female enrolment rose from some 27,000 to 183,000.

At the same time, the government promoted academic mobility to allow students with top grades to acquire further specialization abroad, often in Eastern Europe and the former Soviet Union. They returned to work in scientific and technical fields. It can be said that several hundred thousand women benefited from this training. Some good examples are Wang Shiren, the missile designer, Xiu Guongqiao, the first women to obtain a PhD in science under the new regime, and Xui Minqin, who was associated with the famous Three Gorges engineering project.

Recent Progress

During the 1980s the results of the reform process became visible in the Chinese economy, so there was a growing need for high-level expertise in science and technology to consolidate this success. At the same time, there was a strong emphasis on education, and on retraining the work force.

The progress of women in these spheres was remarkable. According to a national report prepared for the Implementation of the Nairobi Forward-looking Strategies for the Advancement of Women, the illiteracy rate amongst women had dropped from 90% in 1949 to 32% in 1992, and 96% of girls between the ages of 7 and 11 were in school. Moreover, in this same year, girls accounted for 46% of all primary school pupils, 43% of all undergraduate students and 24% of all post-graduate enrolments. In secondary technical schools, girls made up 48.9% of all students - an increase of 10% over the figures for 1985. Between 1985 and 1992, the number of female pupils in secondary vocational schools increased 5% to a total of 46.6%. As well as these impressive advances inside the formal education system, some 9 million women workers received technical training during this period.

In the area of scientific and technical training, women also received special attention. A report entitled **The Situation of Chinese Women** published by the Information Office of the State Council for Science confirmed that the government was pursuing an active policy to ensure training for women scientists and technicians, to improve their living and working conditions, and to promote their involvement in research. As a result, many women have gained prominence in areas such as Physics, Genetic Engineering, Mico-electronics and Space Research. In this last field, more than 400 women currently work at the Xichang satellite centre, many of whom are at the forefront of research. By 1993, the number of women scientists had reached over 8 million which represents some 35% of all workers in this field. Today, in the Chinese Academy of Science, there are 186 women who direct research centres - i.e. nearly 12% of the total. Another 514 (i.e. 14.8%) lead research teams. By 1993, 5.4% of the Chinese Academy of Science were women as 29 had been elected members. A strong non-governmental organization had been founded to represent the interests of women scientists. Today, the China Association for Women Scientists and Technicians has one million members and is affiliated to the All-China Women's Federation.

The 1980s saw women make great strides forward in most scientific fields, including the area of high technology. A good example is the scholar, Wei Yu, who is currently deputy director of the country's State Education Commission, and vice-president of the All-China Women's Federation. She earned a doctorate in Electronics after studies in Germany, and is an award-winning researcher in her field.

Future Perspectives for Women in Science and Technology

Towards Increased Participation

The examples cited have shown that, over the past forty years, many women have entered scientific and technological careers, and through their competence and hard work, they have made outstanding contributions to these areas. Clearly, women equal men in their intellectual ability to pursue research in these fields, nevertheless, their overall participation is lower and their presence at decision-making levels remains much more limited.

Beijing University, the leading national institution of higher learning, presents an interesting study. It has 30 academicians but only 3 (i.e. 10%) are women. A similar trend is clear in professoriate figures which were as follows for 1992:

> 2,000 women professors (10.5%)
> 18,000 women associate professors (2.1%)
> 47,000 women lecturers (30%).

These statistics must improve as quickly as possible, but extremely effective measures will be necessary to bring this about.

Remaining Impediments

Regrettably, a number of factors still exist to impede the educational progress of girls and women.

In the first place, overall school attendance is lower for girls than for boys. Data from the 1990 national census also show that, amongst the remaining 180 million illiterates, 70% are women. The drop-out rate from compulsory schooling is particularly high for girls in poor and rural areas - in fact, it accounts for some 70% of the estimated 10 million in this category over the last ten years.

At the other end of the educational scale, far too few women continue to the highest levels of education, especially in scientific and technical disciplines. In addition, they face discrimination as they must obtain better grades (sometimes up to 30% higher) than boys if they wish to be considered for university selection. The 1992 census showed that there were some 2.2 million students in tertiary-level institutions, 33.7% of whom were female. The 1993 graduation figures reveal that 6,200 women earned Master's degrees (i.e. 2.1% of the total), and 270 obtained a PhD (i.e. 10% of all degrees awarded at this level).

Discrimination is also evident in the area of academic mobility. In 1987, only 602 females out of 3.125 students (i.e. 18.9%) were chosen for studies abroad, according to data supplied by the All-China Women's Federation. Moreover, female students in the Natural Sciences made up only 11.4% of this group.

Furthermore, Chinese women face heavy domestic burdens which hinder their career advancement. China is a developing country where living standards need to be improved and a reduction made in the　number of women in domestic work.

However, Chinese society has traditionally demanded that women assume various personal roles - as daughters, wives, mothers and caregivers - in addition to their professional lives.

In 1985 a survey was conducted by the State Commission for Sciences in a number of municipalities, provinces and regions to investigate households where both husband and wife worked. In both professional and working-class families, the wives undertook all or most of the domestic duties. This clearly presents major problems for women who wish to advance in their chosen careers. In this respect, Science and Technology may constitute a particularly complex problem since an academic career in these fields requires a strong track record in research - hence, a huge investment of personal time is required.

Another very significant factor is attitudinal change amongst women themselves. In China, this is slow in coming. There is considerable pressure for girls to resume domestic duties after completing their studies. Some are discouraged by the difficulties women have in finding attractive career opportunities, while others do not seem to be strongly committed to establishing a career for themselves.

In China, career choices are influenced by the type of secondary studies pursued. Indeed, the small numbers of women in Science and Technology can partly be explained by the direction chosen (which can roughly be described as Arts or Sciences) at the obligatory point during secondary schooling. A simple survey of a typical educational establishment the Beijing First Middle School illustrates this trend for girls to reject the scientific path:

Year	Total of Graduates	Liberal Arts		Sciences/Engineering	
1991	182	38	(23 girls)	144	(56 girls)
1992	91	37	(28 girls)	54	(17 girls)
1993	81	29	(19 girls)	52	(12 girls)
1994	86	43	(23 girls)	43	(19 girls)

Students graduating from this school in 1995 were asked to comment on the continued preference of girls for non-scientific fields. The replies listed a variety of possible explanations:

* the perception of these domains as being difficult discourages students with average or poor grades;
* genuine interest in subjects such as Foreign Languages, Literature and History;
* the belief (rightly or wrongly) that jobs are harder to find with a scientific background but, in contrast, Liberal Arts/Social Science qualifications lead to better-paid careers;
* increased interest in working in the service sector (such as insurance, marketing, banking) where salaries and prospects are considered attractive.

Conclusions

In China, the enhanced participation of women in Science and Technology must be seen in relation to two main facts - firstly, the vast modernization process which has changed the face of society within a short space of time, and secondly, the world-wide problem of limited female presence in these domains.

With regard to the first fact (which constitutes a national priority), China has chosen to adopt measures at the lower levels of education which will surely yield results later. For example, the aim is to eliminate female illiteracy by the year 2000. Another main objective is universal 9-year compulsory education where the drop-out rate for girls should not exceed 2% per year.

Furthermore, the development of vocational and technical education will receive strong emphasis. For the female population, access to on-the-job training for 70% of urban and 50% of rural women by the end of the century is planned.

Such measures will help ensure that the school-age population has adequate exposure to scientific and technical subjects during their basic and secondary education. It will also help women enter the work force in technical and vocational fields. Thus, the right of girls and women to education will be promoted.

As for the second factor, strategies will be devised to promote the interest of female students in scientific and technical domains. This will require not only the stimulation of their enthusiasm, but also a strengthened confidence in their ability to tackle such areas and succeed both in academic and professional careers within them.

To this end, China joins all other countries which are striving to encourage both curricular and pedagogical innovation to ensure that female students are offered the learning options which will equip them to excel in these subjects. While China has produced a great number of brilliant women scientists in a wide variety of disciplines, it - like other countries - no doubt believes that a gender-sensitive approach is justified at all levels of education, including higher learning. Through such measures, the participation of women in Science and Technology - in universities and in tertiary studies overall - may be enhanced.

Gender in Science and Technology: The New Zealand Experience

Robyn Dormer

The University of Auckland, New Zealand

Introduction

Can Science contain a gender dimension? This question should dominate any enquiry regarding women's access to scientific and technological studies and their participation in these domains, notably at the decision-making levels.

Certainly, the overall statistics indicate that the present involvement of women is limited. Moreover, with a few exceptions, till now their career paths in official institutions of science have not been distinguished. It would seem that women work at the periphery of science. This, coupled with the fact that they seldom hold significant numbers of senior positions, means that women cannot guide the future course of this domain.

Women tend to remain excluded from the centre of innovative scientific activity. Here, in the words of the noted American scholar, Evelyn Fox Keller, the goals are the mastery and conquest of nature. In this way, scientific endeavours, which are considered intellectually challenging and complex, become associated with masculine values and prowess. This inevitably leads to the unwelcoming environment known as the "chilly climate" where women are excluded. This professional exclusion on grounds of gender can be further exacerbated by class, race and ethnic factors. Thus, it becomes imperative to recognize the gender dimension of science as a way of encouraging women's increased involvement in its various disciplines.

Special mention must be made of the formative environment of future scientists. It is recognized that even girls who have excelled in science at secondary school can be seriously deterred attitudes are not positive to the point of being gender-sensitive. In general, undergraduate teaching is all too frequently impersonal, and far too little emphasis is placed on the relevance of science in our daily lives. Consequently, it is not surprising that girls find themselves in a cold and unattractive learning situation where one common reaction is to switch courses.

Women and Science in New Zealand - Enrolment Trends

The subsequent data seeks to shed light on some aspects of the New Zealand experience which, in many respects, parallels that of other countries such as the USA.

The University of Auckland
The percentage of women enrolled at the University of Auckland suggest solid but still unequal enrolment by gender in the sciences.

	1992%	1993%	1994%
Botany			
1st year	49	53	53
Masters (4th year)	67	75	52
Geology			
2nd year	24.8	33	30
Masters (4th year)	0	32	26
Chemistry			
1st year	39	41	40
Masters (4th year)	36	30	39
Biochemistry			
2nd year	53	57	63
Masters (4th year)	73	40	30
Computer Science			
2nd year	23	16	19
Masters (4th year)	18	11	8
Physics			
1st year Non-advancing	32	39	31

	1992%	1993%	1994%
1st year Advancing	20	20	25
Masters (4th year)	3	19	14
Masters (4th year)	41	59	49
Pure Mathematics			
1st year Non-advancing	48	48	43
1st year Advancing	33	35	31
Masters (4th year)	17	4	26
Applied Mathematics			
1st year	38	41	43
Masters (4th year)	52	38	34

An analysis of these figures has demonstrated that first-year enrolments tend to reflect the numbers of girls studying scientific subjects at the end of their secondary schooling. Furthermore, in certain domains such as Geology, Computer Science and Physics, special non-advanced courses are offered to encourage enrolment for candidates with a somewhat weaker background knowledge of the field. At this initial stage, percentages are quite steady and balanced in relation to male enrolments.

However, at the Master's level, the statistics reveal lower percentages of female students. These have maintained their interest, but they have become a minority group. This would suggest that the pedagogy of university science may have to make significant progress in order to retain women students who feel able to handle the subjects and are truly at ease in their academic environment.

A total picture of enrolments at the University of Auckland for 1994 and 1995 provides further information on the career choices of women and the balance of students by gender. In both years, women constituted 50% of enrolments.

Table 1
1994 Auckland University Statistics

Course	Total Count	Women Count	Women Percent
BArch	4481	168	34.9%
Bplan	135	63	46.7%
Bprop	148	64	43.2%
BA	6855	4496	65.6%
Bcom	3340	1471	44.0%
BEd	1375	1151	83.7%
BE	1493	239	16.0%
BE(C&M)	185	52	28.1%
BE(Civ)	276	50	18.1%
BE(E&E)	482	75	15.6%
BE(ESc)	120	21	17.5%
BE(M&M)	14	0	0.0%
BE(Mec)	371	30	8.1%
BE(Min)	45	11	24.4%
BFA	256	143	55.9%
LLB	841	437	52.0%
BHB	336	156	46.4%
BMus	152	108	71.1%
BOptum	67	42	62.7%
BSc	3504	1355	38.7%
Btech (BioTech)	25	16	64.0%
Btech (BioMedSc)	26	17	65.4%
Btech (IndMath)	13	2	15.4% (84.6% Asian)
Btech (InfoTech)	74	13	17.6% (50% Asian)
Btech (Materials)	10	1	10.0%
Btech (Optoelect)	42	4	9.5%
TOTAL	26189	13204	50.4%

In 1994, women favoured the Bachelor of Technology degree, notably the Biotechnology option (64%), and the medical science course (65.4%). Engineering enrolments remained low, ranging from 28.1% in the Civil and Mechanical option to 0% in the Metallurgical and Materials course. Studies which require some type of scientific or mathematical talent, such as Architecture and Commerce fared better as they attracted 34.9% and 44% of women.

Table 2
1995 Auckland University Statistics

Course	Total Count	Women Count	Women Percent
BArch	447	167	37.3%
Bplan	150	70	47.0%
Bprop	134	63	47.0%
BA	6399	4150	64.8%
Bcom	3334	1508	45.2%
BEd	1299	1089	83.8%
BE	1423	257	18.1%
BE(C&M)	192	57	29.7%
BE(Civ)	304	69	22.7%
BE(E&E)	427	69	16.1%
BE(ESc)	114	22	19.3%
BE(M&M)	11	2	18.2%
BE(Mec)	346	29	8.4%
BE(Min)	29	9	31.0%
BFA	256	146	57.0%
LLB	870	465	53.4%
BHB	339	154	45.4%
BMus	141	95	67.4%
BOptum	90	60	66.7%
BSc	3440	1310	38.1%
Btech (AniTech)	24	11	78.6%
Btech (BioTech)	44	20	45.5%
Btech (BioMedSc)	52	32	61.5%
Btech (IndMath)	21	6	28.6% (71.4% Asian)
Btech (InfoTech)	117	20	17.6% (52.0% Asian)
Btech (Materials)	27	6	22.0% (51.8% Asian)
Btech (Optoelect)	54	6	11% (44.0% Asian)
TOTAL	25356	12682	%

Legend for Statistics Tables 1 & 2: BArch: Bachelor of Architecture; BPlan: Bachelor of Planning; BProp: Bachelor of Property; BA: Bachelor of Arts; BCom: Bachelor of Commerce; BEd: Bachelor of Education; BE: Bachelor of Engineering; BE(C&M) Chemical and Materials Engineering; BE(Civ) Civil Engineering; BE(E&E) Electrical and Electronics Engineering; BE(ESc) Engineering Science; BE(M&M) Metallurgical and Materials Engineering; BE(Mec) Mechanical Engineering; BE(Min) Mining Engineering; BFA: Bachelor of Fine Arts; LLB: Bachelor of Laws; BHB: Bachelor of Human Biology; BMus: Bachelor of Music; BOptum: Bachelor of Optometry; BSc: Bachelor of Science; (AniTech): Animal Technology;(BioTech): Technology; (BioMedSc): Biomedical Science; (IndMath): Industrial Mathematics; (InfoTech): Information Technology; (Materials): Materials; (Optoelect): Optoelectronics.

Here, a number of subtle and interesting changes are visible. Overall, more women enrolled in the Bachelor of Technology degree, which, itself, expanded options. In addition, the strong presence of female Asian students indicates that this cultural group feels quite confident about scientific degrees, especially those which are mathematics-oriented.

Architecture and Commerce figures remain steady but Engineering continues to attract few women students - less than 20% in each year.

The National Graduation Pattern in 1992
A wider perspective on the number of science and technology degrees awarded would appear to confirm the institutional trends at Auckland University.

Women graduates were significantly fewer in the Natural and Applied Sciences (40%), in Architecture, Town and Resource Planning (30%) and even in Commerce and Business where they earned a little over 50% of all degrees awarded. They became scarce in Engineering (only 10%) and Computing where only 8 out of 53 degrees throughout the country were taken by women.

The overall picture is more positive with a pleasing balance in the total numbers of male and female graduates, and clear parity in the fields of Law and Medicine.

Nevertheless, the scientific domains continue to present challenges and to pose questions for both national and institutional authorities who are striving to fulfil their commitment to the goal of equal access and success for women in relation to their educational opportunities.

Table :   UNIVERSITY DEGREES COMPLETED IN 1992 BY LEVEL OF DEGREE AND ISCED FIELD OF STUDY OF MAIN SUBJECT

ISCED FIELD OF STUDY NUMBER	FIELD OF STUDY	DOCTORATE		MASTERS		BACHELORS HONOURS		BACHELORS		TOTAL		
		male	female	male	female	male	female	male	female	male	female	Total
14	Education	1		35	68			95	421	131	489	620
18	Art, Music & Handcrafts	1		4	9	3	5	66	96	74	110	184
22	Humanities	15	9	147	256	167	234	1126	2173	1455	2672	4127
26	Religion & Theology		2			3	1	26	14	29	17	46
30	Social, Behavioural, Communication Skills	17	12	33	43		9	125	265	175	329	504
34	Commercial & Business	17	1	734	347	333	195	1086	708	2160	1251	3411
38	Law			22	19	87	78	237	251	346	348	694
42	Natural and Applied Sciences	80	27	204	128	207	104	1038	737	1529	996	2525
46	Mathematics	2	1							2	1	3

isced..	field of study	doctorate		masters		bachelors honours		bachelors		total		
		male	female	male	female	male	female	male	female	male	female	Total
48	Computing	7		2	1			36	7	45	8	53
50	Medical & Health	16	11	20	13	5	8	283	239	324	271	595
54	Engineering	25	2	69	12			417	47	511	61	572
58	Architectural, Town Planning, Resource Planning	2		7	1	8	8	165	84	182	93	275
62	Agriculture, Forestry & Fishing	6	2	34	12	26	27	171	111	237	152	389
70	Transport & Communications							4	1	4	1	5
90	Sport & Recreation					7	2	38	53	45	55	100
	Not Stated	10	8							10	8	18
	Total	189	75	1311	909	846	671	4913	5207	7259	6862	14121
	Adjustment for Multiple Completions	1		42	29	64	54	131	98	238	181	419
	NUMBER OF GRADUATES	188	75	1269	880	782	617	4782	5109	7021	6681	13702

Note: This table excludes Diplomas, Certificates and other non-degree progammes.
Source: Education Statistics of New Zealand 1994

The Role of Science in the National Curriculum

In every country, the national curriculum emerges as a vital factor in depicting a vision of science education and its impact on national development objectives. New Zealand is no exception in this regard. A glance at the aims and objectives of science education, as set forth in the New Zealand Curriculum Framework, and at the consideration given to the specific beneficiaries of scientific knowledge and training indicate that a clear gender dimension is not only present but is being actively promoted.

***

General aims of science education, science for all

Science education contributes to the growth and development of all students, as individuals, as responsible and informed members of society, and as productive contributors to New Zealand's economy and future.

The aim of science education in the New Zealand curriculum is to advance learning in science by:
- helping students to develop knowledge and a coherent understanding of the living, physical, material, and technological components of their environment
- encouraging students to develop skills for investigating the living, physical, material, and technological components of their environment in scientific ways
- providing opportunities for students to develop the attitudes on which scientific investigation depends
- promoting science as an activity that is carried out by all people as part of their everyday life
- portraying science as both a process and a set of ideas which have been constructed by people to explain everyday and unfamiliar phenomena
- encouraging students to consider the ways in which people have used scientific knowledge and methods to meet particular needs
- developing students' understanding of the evolving nature of science and technology
- assisting students to use scientific knowledge and skills to make decisions about the usefulness and worth of ideas
- helping students to explore issues and to make responsible and considered decisions about the use of science and technology in the environment
- developing students' understanding of the different ways people influence, and are influenced by, science and technology

- nurturing scientific talent to ensure a future scientific community
- developing students' interest in and understanding of the knowledge and processes of science which form the basis of many of their future careers.

Science education, along with the other essential learning areas, contributes to the development of the essential skills described *in The New Zealand Curriculum Framework (Te Anga Marautanga O Aotearoa)*, Ministry of Education, Wellington, 1993.

Science for All

Science education of the highest standard must be available to all New Zealand students–for those whose formal learning in science will cease when they leave school, for those who develop an interest in a particular aspect of science and may choose a science-related career, and for those who excel at science and may become our future scientists, technologists, technicians, and science educators.

Quality science education for all students requires the removal of barriers to achievement and encourages continuing participation in science. Accordingly, the curriculum in science should recognise, respect, and respond to the educational needs, experiences, achievements, and perspectives of all students: both female and male; of all races and ethnic groups; and of differing abilities and disabilities.

And inclusive curriculum that recognises the perspectives of a particular group of students can enrich education in science for all students.

Girls and Science

Girls can, and do, achieve in science but once they have the choice, many decide not to participate in science courses or seek science-based careers. Many girls view much of school science as outside their life experience and see little use for scientific knowledge and understanding in their future lives.

All students need to feel confident in their ability to succeed. Science education often undervalues the contribution of girls, provides unfamiliar contexts for their learning, and fails to develop their confidence in pursuing studies in this area.

It is important to note that the group "girls" is not homogeneous. Culture and gender factors are inextricably linked and neither should be considered in isolation. The particular perspectives of Maori and Pacific Islands girls should be acknowledged.

A curriculum which is gender-inclusive acknowledges and includes the educational needs and experiences of girls equally with those of boys, both in its content and in the language, methods, approaches, and practices of teaching.

An inclusive curriculum in science provides opportunities for girls to:
- learn science that they value
- develop a range of skills required for successful learning in science
- use their language strengths and co-operative learning skills
- express their experiences, concerns, interests, and opinions
- examine the historical and philosophical construction of science
- view science from a range of perspectives
- interact in an environment where the language and resource materials used are non-sexist
- share the teacher's time and attention equitably with boys.

***

Several aspects of this framework merit close attention, namely:
- the linkage between science and environment:

- the encouragement of the skills required for scientific investigation to advance the frontiers of knowledge;

- the articulation of an inclusive curriculum which recognizes the perspectives of various groups of students;

- the expression of confidence in the ability of girls to pursue scientific studies;

- due emphasis on the history and philosophy of science which serve to better illustrate its applications;

- the right of girls to fully equal opportunities with boys in the selection and enjoyment of scientific courses.

Such guidelines go a considerable distance towards recognizing that major barriers definitely persist and are preventing high achievement by females in science-oriented studies. These barriers must and can be removed by clear and equitable policy statements which explicitly promote the gender dimension and thus open the way forward to genuinely equal educational opportunity.

Conclusions

The purpose of these observations has been to illustrate that one country's trends at the national and institutional levels tend to find similar patterns in other regional contexts. What is clear is that the overall challenge of improving the access and participation of women in scientific and technological disciplines embraces a variety of issues - each complex in its own manner. For this reason, extreme caution must be exercised to avoid false or marginal questions.

Thus, to conclude this sketch of the New Zealand context, it might be useful to suggest three areas where the gender dimension of science and technology can be practically advanced:

Linkages between National and Institutional Policy-making

This helps ensure that those specific issues pertaining to each particular country have been clearly identified and are being effectively tackled by policy-makers and the academic community together. This collaboration can target a dual outcome:

- on the one hand, national policy frameworks can be properly articulated;
- on the other, the guiding principles and objectives of national policy can be applied at grass-roots level by institutions of higher learning which have pledged to help encourage women students to enter the scientific professions.

Harmonization of the Global and Local Perspectives

Today global issues cannot be forgotten as the pace of social change dictates that national issues be sited within a wider arena. This perspective highlights areas such as:

- gender and science in formal and non-formal educational systems;

- the interaction between women, science and the environment which may have particular relevance in the developing world;
- the challenges in interpreting data on gender and science and the difficulty associated with this numerical analysis. Professor Anne Hibner Koblitz, an American consultant to the Statistical Division of the United Nations, captures this issue well when she observes:

> "Women's experiences in the sciences, technology and medicine across disciplines, cultures and historical periods, have been diverse and often show contradictory tendencies. We should therefore be extremely hesitant to make sweeping generalizations about the female nature or women's roles under patriarchy. The interactions of gender, culture and science are complex; it is unwise to draw simplistic conclusions that stereotype women's participation and status in the sciences."[1]

Caution is thus advised to ensure that the right remedy is chosen for the particular gender problem at hand.

Advocacy by Non-governmental Organizations
The advocacy role of NGOs is one of their best-known functions. Their impact in raising public awareness has been of the greatest importance and this includes the gender dimension of science. Due to their promotion of key goals, - such as equal access to S and T fields, enhanced understanding of the applications of science, and the assurance of a critical mass of women scientists in decision-making roles, as well as focus on the social benefits to be derived from women's scientific knowledge, - they have established their voice in international fora where the gender dimension of S and T is debated. Every effort must be made to permit these NGOs to continue their role as advocates of progress for women scientists.

If action can be ongoing in these three fields, then the gender dimension of science will become better understood and supported. One may hope that the ultimate result will be that the boundaries of scientific knowledge are pushed ahead by male and female scientists in more equal numbers and with a common concern to place science at the service of society.

Notes

1. Hibner Koblitz Anne. "Global Perspectives - Challenges in interpreting data" in *The Gender Dimension of Science and Technology*. UNESCO, Paris 1995.

The author thanks Elizabeth Godfrey, University of Auckland for assistance with statistical data.

Bibliography

Fox Keller, Evelyn. "Gender and Science" in *Discovering Reality*, edited by Sandra Harding and Merrill B. Hintikka, London, 1983.

UNESCO. *The Gender Dimension of Science and Technology*. Paris, 1995.

The New Zealand Curriculum Framework: Te Anga Marautanga o Aotearoa. Ministry of Education, Wellington, 1993.

Public Administration

Maria Teresa Gallego and Otilia Mó
Universidad Autónoma de Madrid, Spain

Introduction

Spanish women have come a long way towards equality in a very short time. In just one decade (1978-88) they have passed from an era which kept them in silence and subordination, to one where their rights are comparable with those of other European women. But, in real terms, their equality with men still seems remote in terms of the balanced participation of both sexes in all fields of society.

Today, legislation against sexual discrimination exists. This resulted from the work of the feminist movements in the sixties and seventies, together with the support obtained from international organizations, and the general move in favour of gender equality. Thus, the issue of legal equality may be considered settled. Nevertheless, even in the most developed societies, serious imbalances continue to be found between men and women. To eliminate these and to allow women to realize their full potential and so enjoy a better way of life, (which will benefit society in general), further changes related to gender matters are still necessary.

Since 1979, centres for Women's Studies have existed at Spanish universities, and have carried out systematic work to analyse the creation and transmission of knowledge marked by androcentrism. Attempts have been made to introduce changes in the academic curriculum, but without great success. It is possible to carry out research and teaching from the point of view of women, but this must be harmonized with the academic requirements of the various faculties. It must be said that, for the present, it is practically impossible to make significant changes in

191

this area.[1] One of the main reasons for this is women's lack of power in the university structure. They are rarely in control of universities, faculties or departments. Moreover, they make up only 10% of high-level teaching staff, and approximately 30% of all university teaching staff.

It is necessary to take this reality into account when analyzing the curriculum in Public Administration, where gender aspects are not considered to any significant degree. By Public Administration, we mean the academic training required for the Civil Service which is responsible for the implementation of government policy in any state - and thus for its social and economic development. Furthermore, it should be remembered that the role of universities has long been influenced by our political history. The development of special courses in the field of gender has not been a high priority. In fact, the introduction of such studies in Public Administration has been so recent and limited, that it does not allow us to refer to any specific case in any university. For this reason, it will be necessary to describe the situation in a more general way.

Teaching Public Administration in Spain

In the early 1940s, the Faculty of Politics, Economics and Commerce was established at Madrid's Complutense University. This was the only one of its kind which existed in Spain until the end of the eighties. It had just one specific goal: to train staff for the state bureaucracy and, at the same time, to support the government. From the seventies onwards, this university gained a new focus. A great number of its students and teachers used their knowledge to critically question government policy.

The Politics curriculum had a marked legal character, more than anything else. Consequently, Public Administration consisted of Administrative Law, and Public and Constitutional Law. This last area had to be taught from a comparative point of view, as Spain had yet to adopt its own Constitution.[2]

After the transition to constitutional government, major changes took place. For example, the Law for University Reform (i.e. LUR) passed in 1983 allowed Politics to be studied in various courses, as new faculties in different universities were set up. For the first time, the area of knowledge known as Politics and Administration was established. Therefore, Public Administration, per se, was never really a discipline in its own right in the Spanish university structure. It was taught as a part of the Politics curriculum. It should be said that this situation is not completely atypical, as Public Administration can be certainly studied from the standpoints of Law and Sociology, as well as from that of Politics.

During this time, gender issues were absent from the curricula.

In contrast, from the mid-eighties onwards, Public Administration began to receive great attention inside the Politics curriculum, which was expanded and enriched by the addition of much more diverse material. This change was driven by the need to modernize the country and its social structures. Although the concept of modernization is frequently mentioned on the international scene, in Spain it is a reality rather than mere rhetoric. There was an urgent necessity to introduce new systems of organization, management and communication. In particular, people had to be trained differently, so the whole field of Human Resources became vital. This modernization was not due to internal demands, as the Spanish Civil Service was fully professional. Rather, it resulted from the changing times and social context which called for a restructuring of the Spanish state.

Once again the historic reasons are very significant. Since the start of constitutional government,[3] successive governments have talked about the unresolved problem of reform in the field of

Public Administration - despite the fact that quite considerable change has occurred. Since 1983, Spain has been divided into seventeen regions, each with a very different level of transfer of responsibilities from the central administration. Also, local administration encountered its own problems, which were economic in character. Generally speaking therefore, further adaptation of the different administrations is still required so that they can tackle present problems effectively.

In response to this, Political Science curricula have tried to develop teaching and research which deal with different types of issues presented by administration at the central, regional and local levels. In a very short space of time, the traditional legal and administrative standpoint has been extended to the important areas of management, taxation, budget control, sectoral policy analysis, health, environment and other such aspects related to social policy. In these faculties, a case study approach may be favoured in order to present the current nature of the material. However, the introduction of this is still fairly recent and limited. Particular schools of thought and definite trends have not yet emerged.

In Spain, the need to adapt public structures and systems to the demands and requirements of citizens is duly recognized - just as it is in any other democratic and developed society. Because of this, new undergraduate degrees have been created in some universities over the past few years.[4] For example, there is a Diploma in Management and Public Administration, which takes three years and allows access to the second cycle of the Political Science programme.

So far, we have given a brief description of the curriculum studies related to Public Administration now available in Spanish universities. In addition, we have sought to identify the presence of gender questions in the education of these future civil servants. It can be confirmed that there are no disciplines treating gender issues explicitly. However, it might be possible that these are included in certain fields such as Human Resources,[5] Public Policy, or perhaps those related to the analysis of political parties and social movements. Of course, gender issues may be assumed to be present in some teachers' personal attitudes. But, there are no cases of this area appearing in subject or course titles.

Very often, modernization deals with more structural and systemic issues. Here, clear orientations concerning course content and the approaches used by teachers can be noted. On the one hand, key topics include the structural components of public administration, its social structure, linkages with the political elite and the analysis of its routine procedure. On the other hand, there is a strong focus on the activity of various types of administration, including their decision-making procedures, and the analysis of the results obtained by these bodies.[6] This means that traditional theory is balanced with a more applied approach, which combines analysis of public policies and their range of applications to management. Problem-solving is considered to be a useful pedagogical method to study the process of modernization within the sphere of Spanish public administration - a domain, we should add, which needs to improve its results and its image in the eyes of citizens.

Spain has one autonomous organization with important functions of co-ordination, advice, training and selection related to Public Administration, namely the Instituto Nacional de Administración Pública (INAP).[7] This is responsible for the selection of civil servants who will work in state and local governments. For both these areas, a national degree is awarded. Apart from the initial selection by means of an entry examination, INAP is responsible for in-service training, (whether regular or specialized), for civil servants. For this purpose, it offers a large number of basic and specific courses for the different branches and levels of the Spanish Civil Service.[8]

Changing Academic Approaches

As we have pointed out, as recently as four years ago, there was no university degree in Public Administration in Spain. Even now, the only one which exists is at the undergraduate level. University graduates from a variety of disciplines (e.g. Law, Politics and Sociology) can take the entry exam for the Civil Service. Once selected, the INAP deals with their formal training as civil servants.[9]

Since 1991, INAP has organized a special post-graduate course in Public Administration in co-operation with the Ortega and Gasset University Institute. This course focuses on the process of modernization and deals, inter alia, with the use of new technologies such as management tools so as to better satisfy the demands of citizens, who are now considered to be clients.

While this demonstrates that curricular change is beginning to take place, there is still no real emphasis on the gender dimension at the present time - either in this particular post-graduate curriculum or in other specialized courses.

However, a few programmes with this dimension do, in fact, exist. One is to be run on the design and application of public policy-making and programmes to ensure equal opportunities for women. This will have 17 hours teaching time and will be limited to 25 participants. The course was set up in collaboration with the Women's Institute,[10] a governmental organization for the promotion of gender equality. There are also three officially approved courses, each of which lasts 15 hours, related to the training of civil servants. These also deal with equal opportunities for women and are run by the "Comisiones Obreras" or Trade Unions.[11]

Notwithstanding these rare cases, it is true to say that both the university curriculum and the specialized training carried out by INAP lack any clearly defined gender dimension. If we consider the presence of women in the field of Public Administration, the fact that this issue has not been raised by those responsible for course design in this area seems strange. After all, 42% of all civil servants in Public Administration are women - though at the upper levels, this drops to just 25% and in the most responsible posts, such as division and section heads, they make up around 12%.[12] As might be expected, practically half of the administrative and secretarial staff are women, but their participation in posts of responsibility and decisions is much smaller. Nowadays, no one can imagine the domain of Public Administration without the participation of women. Quite simply, it is not possible to manage without their contribution. Yet, at the decision-making levels, they are very few in number. Hopefully this will change, since the principle of equality - now widely respected - requires that they be given the same opportunities as their male colleagues.[13]

Because women occupy mainly the base of the pyramid and are rarely present at the top of the professional ladder, the gender imbalance in Civil Service careers can be explained. This is not due to any inferiority in terms of women's training or capacities. In Spain, women make up more than 50% of university students and they achieve a high level of success when competing in the entry exam for this career.[14] However, when the question of promotion to a post of responsibility arises, their success rate is very reduced. Sadly, this constitutes not only a grave injustice, but also a waste of potential that modern societies cannot afford. Without doubt, the university curriculum could be a useful means of changing this situation if a gender element were included to emphasize the importance of women's role in the process of social development.

It seems incomprehensible that such issues continue to be absent from the two fields of training for Public Administration careers that exist in Spain - namely, universities and the INAP. This training remains strongly influenced by the bureaucratic model, which, in reality, is not neutral but profoundly masculine .[15] Still harder to understand are the continuous appeals for the modernization of public structures which do not include rational elements about gender issues. Although this dimension has been partially taken into consideration at the level of local administration, notably via the creation of posts to promote the equality of opportunities for women,[16] much still remains to be accomplished.

A description of the current situation illustrates that the Public Administration curriculum in Spanish universities is in a transitional phase. While it is true to say that from about 1985 onwards Politics faculties started to change and to develop their own identity with regard to the study of Public Administration, really innovative courses in Management and Public Administration are still very recent as they were established only at the beginning of the 1990s.

Overall, when it comes to designing the curriculum, the introduction of specific subjects dealing with gender issues, is not being considered on a sufficiently wide scale. In Political Science at Madrid's Complutense University, there is only one subject entitled "Women and Power Relations", which explicitly analyses such questions. Another is "Gender Theories"[17] which is part of the Political Science degree at the Universidad Autónoma de Madrid. This 60-hour course introduces students to the main components of Feminist Theory so that they may be better sensitized to gender issues in relation to the formulation of social policy. In this way, it is hoped that future civil servants will have a broader - and improved - attitude to matters which have particular significance for women in society.

Another reason that can explain the lack of interest in gender issues is the current profile of the university teaching staff. In the disciplines of Political Science and Public Administration, women constitute just 18.6% of the whole professoriate, and only two (i.e. 7.1%) are chairholders. Thus, from the quantitative standpoint, we can see that there have been very few opportunities to influence the introduction of gender issues in these academic programmes. Till fairly recently, the feminist movement in Spain has proved to be very distant from questions related to the political system and from the political agenda itself. Fortunately, it can be said that this view is changing and that there are now more possibilities to articulate the specific requirements of women and to make provision for these within the political system. As this continues to grow, it must take due account of the numerous issues in the field of Public Administration which affect women in all walks of life.

Conclusion

Today, it is both desirable and essential to introduce an awareness of the reality of women's lives in all areas of the university curriculum. This is a principle which deserves to be reiterated. Such sensitization should be promoted via case studies which deal with women's development, and via theory to help explain the inequalities which they can still face. The curriculum must also help seek solutions by including adequate analysis and concrete examples as to how women can develop their potential - both for their own benefit and for that of society as a whole.

In the specific field of Public Administration, these changes have become crucial because each and every state is increasingly required to address itself to women in terms of their rights and needs - both as citizens and as members of the work force. Spain is no exception in this instance.

Notes

1.   Ballaring P., Gallego M. T. and Martínez M. I. *Libro Blanco de Estudios de la Mujeres en las Universidades Españolas 1975-1991*. (To be published).

2.   The Spanish professor, García Pelayo, did important work in the area of Constitutional Law while at Caracas University, Venezuela.

3.   The first elections after Franco's death took place in 1977 and the Spanish Constitution was ratified in 1978.

4.   These exist in 8 out of 44 universities. The Universidad Autónoma de Barcelona offers a Master's Degree in Public Management. At this institution, professors from the course entitled Seminari d'Etudis de la Dona have offered a seminar on Sexual Inequality and Social Policy which is integrated into the general course on this latter subject.

5.   Professor Blanca Olias de Lima, a Political Science and Administration specialist, is thanked for her comments on this point. She currently offers a course on Human Resources where she personally introduces gender issues, but confirms that no specific programme on this topic is taught.

6.   Subirats, Joan. "La Administraciòn Pùblica." In R. Cotarelo. *Ciencia Política y de la Administración*. Ed. Complutense, pp 63-65, 1994.

7.   This was created in 1987, merging the School of Public Administration and the Centre for the Study of Local Administration.

8.   The Galician and Catalan Schools of Public Administration are recently created institutions. Others may also exist.

9.   During the first term of 1995, the INAP offered more than 30 specialized courses to middle-level civil servants. Subjects included Public Management, Human Resources, Administrative Procedures.

10.   INAP Archives 1994, p.109

11.   Ibid p.116

12.   Women are in the majority in the following ministries: Public Administration 63.5%, Culture 66.4%, Security 65%, Social Affairs 56.3%, Health 55.2%. In others, they represent about 50%. These figures do not include the teaching profession, the national security forces (which admitted women after 1988), or the Ministries of Justice and Social Security. Source: *La Mujer en Cifras*, Women's Rights Institute, 1992 p.61 onwards.

13. Valcarcel, Amelia. El Techo de Cristal. Obstacles for women's political participation. In *Las Mujeres y El Poder Político.* Women's Rights Institute, Debate Series 16. 1994. This discusses feminism as an ideology and in management discourse.

14. In recent years, more women can be found in legal field. The first women judge was appointed in 1971. In 1995, women represented over 40% of the judicature and more than 30% of the staff in the Public Prosecutor's office. There is no woman on the Supreme Court.

15. A good reference is Stivers, Camilla. *Gender Images in Public Administration. Legitimacy and the Administrative State.* Sage Publications. 1993.

16. The first course was organized by the Women's Rights Institute (a government agency) in 1991. In 1992, the first meeting of Equal Opportunity officers was held and a network founded with support from national and international bodies.

17. The curriculum in Political Science and Management and Public Administration was examined at the following universities: the autonomous universities of Madrid and Barcelona, Complutense, Carlos III, UNED, Pompeu Fabra. The INAP archives were consulted and professors in various departments were asked for information.

Gender in Demography and Population Studies at University Level

Mouna L. Samman
UNESCO

Introduction

Demography is the science which permits the study of human populations and their evolution. It also covers the interface between demographic, economic and social phenomena, as well as the study of demographic theories and doctrines which serve as the foundation for population policies. The final objective of such policies is the human development process. No course in History, Geography, Sociology, Economics or Biology can really ignore references to Demography. Mastery of this field "allows understanding of many other areas."[1]

As a discipline, Demography has developed in tandem with major conferences on population issues organized by the United Nations - the Cairo meeting in September 1994 being the most recent. These conferences have played a major role in the exchange of information and in the sensitization and mobilization of decision-makers as well as of the international research community. Such conferences have recommended that training programmes in population and population-related studies be strengthened. Moreover, they have invited governments to develop an adequate core of trained persons for the formulation and implementation of integrated population and development policies, plans and programmes. In particular, the last-mentioned should take place at all levels of education.

At the same time, it should be remembered that a much better international understanding of demographic problems came about largely as a result of the censuses and their analysis in developing countries. These exercises, starting in the 1960s, have been further expanded to almost all these countries. Finally, the launching of the World Fertility Survey (WFS) in the 1970s, and the Demographic and Health Surveys (DHS) in the 1980s and 1990s facilitated the collection of comparable data in more than 40 developing countries. This gave rise to an in-depth analysis of the main factors and variables related to individual or collective demographic behaviour.

Progress in research and the consolidation of the demographic knowledge base have affected the teaching of Demography in universities - even if the teaching of this discipline is a little less advanced in the developing nations where it constitutes a rather new field. About 15 years ago, these countries felt a great need for trained personnel in Demography which led to a great expansion of teaching in this discipline. This expansion was also requested by many opinion streams which were anxious about the rapid population growth in these countries. Another noticeable trend has been a multi- or inter-disciplinary approach to training in order to underscore the relevance of population variables in relation to a broad range of important social development issues.

At the present time, Demography is generally taught at the first and second levels of university degrees as a component of Bachelor and Master's programmes in Sociology, Anthropology, Geography, Economics, Statistics and Public Health. Demography as a primary subject is much less common - rather it is a credit or optional course.[2] Specialized programmes which provide a specific degree or qualification in Demography are only found at the post-graduate level of education.

The Role of the Teacher

While teaching Demography may require reference to complex theories and the use of numerous statistical data, this field really concentrates on basic and universal subjects such as birth, illness, death, marriage and family. In all of these, the role and conditions of the actors differ according to their sex. Hence, gender is - and has always been - one of the key variables used in demographic analysis. And yet, in most cases, teaching programmes contain neither the issue of sexual equality nor those questions related to the condition of women in this era. The analysis undertaken simply states sexual differences - in particular, the specific characteristics involved with perhaps a few sociological references to the situations studied.

In this context, it is important to emphasize the role of the teacher. It is generally agreed that, even when a course has a lot of scope for discussing women and gender issues, the actual level of analysis attained tends to depend on the gender sensitivity of the instructor. Of course, it is true that Demography is, in itself, neutral, and that it is not the role of university teaching to recommend either social - and still less - feminine models of behaviour. Nevertheless, it must be recognized that the description or interpretation of observable facts and of their changing nature are influenced to a large degree by the approach of each particular teacher. This person can promote a particular ideology or viewpoint - for example, by highlighting or by avoiding certain issues and by the selection of the material taught which might include international comparisons to justify his or her remarks.

It is interesting to note that, generally speaking, men and women teachers demonstrate different attitudes when dealing with gender issues.[3] Although men are now well sensitized to problems of discrimination based on sex, they usually adopt a conciliatory tone when facing conflictual subjects - thereby avoiding any debate on the complex question of sexual equality. On the other hand, women are more concerned about this very point and tend to insist on the public and private roles to be played by women. In particular, they resist any attempt to categorize this sex as wives and mothers exclusively. It should also be noted that women are so poorly represented in the teaching profession in many countries that their impact on the nature and rate of social change is minimal.

This paper studies how university teaching in Demography deals with issues related to women and gender in relation to two countries - Egypt[4] and India.[5] The remarks will be based on case studies undertaken. Of course, analysis of content alone cannot extend to the pedagogical processes involved - these are vital as they really demonstrate the complexity of the questions under scrutiny. In the two countries studied, the primary concern is that of demographic growth and its impact on socio-economic development. In these countries, teaching content is strongly influenced by ideological considerations - since the population preoccupation is very old, and reflects political attitudes to the population issue. The two specific case studies define Demography sufficiently widely to include courses which examine its economic and social aspects. Thus, Population Geography, Population Policy, Population and Socio-economic Planning all figure alongside more traditional courses in the theory and method of Demography.

Gender Issues in the Teaching of Demography

Studying the evolution of a given population requires an analysis of phenomena related to its growth or decline and the repercussions of this in terms of age and gender, marriage, fertility, mortality and migration, as well as of socio-professional structure and activity rates. In this general context, women are held primarily responsible for population increase. This is unfair but explains why they receive special attention in the study of relevant phenomena, as we shall see below.

The composition of the population by sex and age groups are standard parts of most demographic analysis. The sex ratio often demonstrates an imbalance between numbers of men and women but consideration is not always given to key variables behind these imbalances, such as differential migration patterns, high levels of maternal and infant mortality, female deficits due to differential abortions and so on. The consequences of this imbalance could affect the matrimonial cycle, though this result is not generally recognized.

When talking about population structure and composition, the question of gender in a household is included: for example, the number of couples in the household or the instance of female-headed households. However, no special provisions exist in any programme to specifically examine gender and legal status within the household and family. Here, important issues include marriage and polygamy, conditions for divorce and separation, child custody and inheritance rights. In India, where a women's status in the household is very much associated with the amount of dowry she brings at the time of marriage, tradition is paramount in family matters. In Egypt, questions relating to the personal conditions of the man and the women are considered the private domain of the family. Therefore, these types of issues are not subjects for debate in university courses. Moreover, because of their religious and ideological character, very few researchers - let alone teachers - have been able to explore these topics.

Fertility and Mortality

In studying fertility determinants, attention is currently given to changing social factors, such as the social status of women, the value of children, the marked preference for male children, and other factors of a psychological, economic or cultural nature which can motivate or influence reproduction.

The link between **the educational level of a woman and her reproductive behaviour** is a fairly recurrent theme, which is encountered in all courses on population dynamics. The impact of women's education on reproductive behaviour is discussed at two levels - how different levels of education affect the age of marriage and how they affect the total fertility rate. In Egypt and India, where it is strongly advocated that children should be born in wedlock, a later marriage age has a truncation effect on marital fertility. Moreover, the role of education in encouraging child spacing and the use of contraceptives is very evident in India. But the decline in the mean number of children in the family is not perceived to be a factor which could permit women to assume new roles in society and actively participate in the social and economic spheres. In fact, both India and Egypt recommend greater access to education for women - so as to equal that of men. Yet, in reality, improving women's education seems to be tackled in terms of population policy rather than as a need or fundamental right for all people.

Tradition, culture and religion have an enormous impact on fertility, and this is currently mentioned in courses on population. The impact is particularly true in rural societies, which represent 74% and 56% of the population in India and Egypt respectively.   The practices which still continue in these societies place women in a very difficult situation. For example, in India, women are not in control of their fertility which is largely determined by mothers-in-law or relatives. In Egypt, the social status of a woman is largely determined by the number of children that she produces, - and especially the number of male children. This emphasis on the number of children, including males, could be one reason why women strive to have as many children as possible. This also encourages women to be totally dependent on their husbands, as they tend to fear repudiation or polygamy.

In Egypt, fertility is considered to be linked to a family's status. The nuclear families have a rather low fertility level, and the extended families a higher one. Nuclear families are mostly situated in the urban zones, while patriarchal families predominate in rural areas. In these type of families, the father has absolute authority, the boys are more valued than the girls, and the women are not associated with the important decisions taken within the family. Early marriage for girls is encouraged, while their education is not.

The official population policy in India has been in force for some forty years, and every Population Studies programme in the country has a full course (or major part of a course) devoted to fertility knowledge and family planning. In this area men are rarely concerned, while the women are the focus because the majority of the current methods of contraception are directed towards them. Indeed, since the early 1970s, male sterilization has greatly decreased, the utilization of condoms has been replaced by the IUD and the pill and it is estimated that about 96 per cent of the total sterilizations are female. When raising contraception issues in a university course, discussions on the methods available and their uses are studied with regard to their impact on the reduction of fertility. In this context, one would be tempted to wonder whether fertility regulation programmes in India are really working to favour the cause of women. According to the opinion of a respected Indian specialist[6] the way these programmes are implemented has rather helped to perpetuate traditional social norms and sexual discrimination. For him, it is "a pernicious combination of tradition and technology".

This means that instead of being an essential element in the process of women's emancipation, the family planning programme is now a source of inequality between the sexes within the context of population change.

The legal aspect of induced abortion is studied in India in the framework of the 1972 Medical Termination of Pregnancy Act. This includes its impact on fertility. The use of abortion as a measure of sex selection, particularly amongst the generally educated middle class, is also highlighted. Indeed, misuse of amniocentesis and other prenatal diagnostic tests that allow for sex determination of the unborn child lead to an increasing number of abortions when they reveal that the unborn child is female. Some recent data in India showed, for example that there are now 110 boys born for 100 girls, while the normal sex ratio is 105 boys for every 100 girls. It goes without saying that these foeticides represent the most extreme form of discrimination against one half of the population and thus it is desirable and necessary to eliminate this practice as quickly as possible.

An analysis of the mortality rate emphasizes the difference in the life expectancy at birth between men and women. The educational level of the mother is a crucially important factor in the reduction of infant and juvenile mortality. Furthermore, in India, the education of women is now considered to be vital to the health of all family members and is given due attention in the teaching process. Nevertheless, the mortality rate of female children is exceptionally high and is aggravated by malnutrition and the lack of necessary care. It would appear that more attention could be given to this aspect.

After the International Conference on Population and Development (Cairo 1994), the issue of women's reproductive health gained greater importance worldwide. In addition to contraception and abortion, the new approach covers topics such as reproductive rights, sexually transmitted diseases including HIV/AIDS and sexual behaviour. In India, reproductive health is now being discussed under the heading of maternal mortality, with a focus on the health of women who are of child-bearing age. However, many countries are not yet including the question of gender and STD/AIDS in Population Studies courses - which is unfortunately the case for both India and Egypt. Another important subject which is not given much consideration is excision - i.e. female genital mutilation. This is still practised on young girls in a number of countries and in deplorable hygienic conditions.

Women in Professional Activity

Available statistics, obtained from censuses and specific studies, suggest that the professional activities of women are seriously underestimated. Hence, the figures on working women are generally inaccurate. This is true, for example, in the agricultural area and in the small family businesses. While this lacuna might be mentioned in certain academic courses in India, the contribution of women to the GNP is not sufficiently evident - either via adequate research studies or as a dimension of the teaching programme. In addition, the fact that only few women have access to national production resources, both in Egypt and India, is not highlighted. These resources destined to stimulate the productive sector are predominantly controlled by men. This situation is partly due to the laws governing inheritance, in which property rights are transferred from father to son. But it also stems from very ancient traditions which prevent women from reclaiming what is rightly theirs, and explains the preference for male children, which is common in patriarchal societies. Consequently, women are in a very weak position both socially and legally. Yet, physically, their fertility is maintained at a very high level.

The quantitative increase of women in paid employment is presented in the two countries under study as proof of the improvment in the status of the female sex. Moreover, it is also a factor to indicate lower fertility rates. It is true that there is a clear correlation between the contacts women have with the outside world, notably in their relationships outside the family circle, and the impact of these on their reproductive patterns. However, if society continues to encourage women to participate in economic activity solely to put pressure on their time and to limit the number of children they bear, the real "emancipation" of women - and certainly their fulfilment - are not advanced. Fertility rates will surely be reduced but real equality between the sexes will not be improved.

In the study on employment, the level of activity is presented by sex along with gender distribution by sectors of activity. Yet, it is very rare to analyse socio-professional structures, which often demonstrate that women are mostly engaged in subordinate employment. Furthermore, nothing is said about aspects such as employment opportunities, equality of access and job security. In this context, when explaining unemployment amongst young women in the 15 to 24 age group in Egypt, it is argued that more and more women are seeking employment but employers are hesitant to engage them. Repeated absenteeism of women at the workplace, due to family responsibilities, and the excessive legislation which protects them, are also sources of complaint for employers. However, the complex challenges faced by women who must balance their family and professional responsibilities are seldom acknowledged.

The informal sector in Egypt and India has played a dominant role in each country's economy in terms of creating jobs. Apart from agriculture, many women are to be found in informal work - in manufacturing, trade or commerce, transportation or in the service sector. The social and legal status of these women is rarely considered, and their contribution to the family income is not fully recognized.

When migration is studied, age and the gender are important elements. In Egypt, studies have been done to assess the consequences for women of male migration to the Gulf states - here, the impact in both the sending and receiving countries are analysed. The departure of the male members of the family means that additional responsibilities fall on women, especially in the lower classes of society. However, there is little improvement in their social status or independence since these women are often placed in the charge of another male member of the family in the absence of their own father, husband or son.

Conclusion

The preceding analysis is intended to give a current picture of the trends governing university teaching in Demography in Egypt and India. Clearly, some differences exist between these countries and a certain inequality between the sexes is evident in both. However, the perspective is now becoming more open so that a significant break with the traditions of the past is beginning to emerge. This suggests that there is a common purpose in both nations to accord women a role in society which is better recognized - even if they are still considered to be the main beneficiaries of these changes rather than active partners and agents in the process itself.

Whether these efforts have a positive effect on students is very hard to assess since attitudinal change is slow and delicate to evaluate. Moreover, students are exposed to a variety of other sources of information to increase their knowledge and perhaps to alter their views. Of course, this information comes principally via the multi-media which brings an international perspective. At the same time, the return to the fundamentalist stance in relation to morality and religion is a strong and influential trend throughout the world.

The profile of women in this context is ambiguous if not paradoxical - **a juxtaposition of modernism and conservatism** - the latter being especially evident in private life. The fact of being engaged in paid work outside the home is regarded more as an economic necessity rather than an achievement - this is even the view of the women involved. Although they may be better educated, women now are no less dependent on men - either because of tradition or the law. Women are not yet the masters of their own destiny and are not really aware of their active role in the process of economic and social change. This is clearly reflected in India and Egypt which are now undergoing a state of transition. Furthermore, the controversy concerning the status of women is definitely one of the main issues in all the different ideologies which are to be found in these countries.

Full equality between the sexes is still very far in the future. Universities can contribute to the elimination of prejudices, and should study the best ways to achieve this goal. For example, these institutions could lead a reflection on the new options open to women for the choice and management of their lives. This would inevitably contrast new and progressive legal measures with older and more restrictive practices based on tradition. At the same time, it could serve to emphasize that women must first have a clear image of their own improved status. Without this, there is no point in urging men to alter their traditional viewpoints with regard to women.

Even if universities have an open approach to social change and modern thinking, their numbers are somewhat too limited to ensure that major transformation will occur rapidly. However, one area where they can have considerable impact is in the training of secondary teachers. If the curriculum has included the promotion of sexual equality and equity issues, then these professionals can transmit such principles through their teaching. The first International Congress on Population Education and Development, organized by UNESCO and the United Nations Fund for Population Activities and held in Istanbul in April 1993, clearly recognized the critical role of the university in this domain:

"Universities have a significant advisory role to play in the training of educational personnel, and especially in regard to research, the design of programmes for teacher trainers and the preparation of materials."[7]

In the light of these words, it is obvious that universities have a major responsibility to include the gender dimension in curriculum renovation and that they must respond to this challenge with commitment and energy.

Notes

1   "L'enseignement de la démographie", par Michel Louis Levy, *Population et Sociétés, no. 239*, INED, Paris, octobre 1989.

2.   "Teaching Demography" - a summary handlist of Universities and other Institutions Teaching Demography - Vol. 5, United Nations, New York, 1985.

3.   Bella, N. *L'enseignement des questions de population à l'Université et l'importance accordée au genre*, Etude de cas sur France, mars 1995.

4.   Morcos, W. "L'enseignement des questions de population à l'Université et l'importance accordée au genre", Etude de cas sur l'Egypte, avril 1995.

5.   Premi, K. *Gender issues in Population Studies Curricula at University level*, Study case of India, May 1995.

6.   Bose, A. "Gender issues and Population Change: Tradition, Technology and Social Turbulence", in *International Social Science*

Journal, Sept. 1994, no. 141, "Population: issues and policies", UNESCO.

Ashish Bose was professor and head of the Population Research Centre, Institute of Economic Growth, Delhi. Author of several books and research papers. Currently, he member of the Expert Group on Population Policy set up by the Government of India.

7.   Extract from the "Action Framework for Population Education on the Eve of the Twenty-First Century", in the Final Report of the First International Congress on Population Education and Development, Istanbul, 14-17 April 1993.

The Gender Dimension in Agronomy: A Student Perspective

Willemijn Tuinstra
International Association of Agricultural Students (IAAS)

Introduction

The student is, of course, one of the most important stakeholders in higher education. Students have a direct interest in the design of the university curriculum. Therefore, in this chapter, the International Association of Agricultural Students (IAAS) would like to express a student viewpoint on the gender dimension in Agronomy.

The nature of this chapter will probably be a little different from others in the book. We are not really experts on the gender issue, but we can illustrate how we feel involved in this. In particular we want to show how an international student organization can function as a platform for intercultural exchange, stimulate discussion on an international level, and encourage concrete action. We have experienced that we can learn a lot from each other, even just by sitting together and talking about the reality of life in different countries.

We think that it is essential to involve students in curriculum development, because they can often draw attention to neglected issues. In this case, we are focusing on the gender issue. In agriculture, the role of women is of the utmost importance, but sadly, very frequently underestimated.

This chapter is not a case-study on the situation in one particular country or university, as Ihave preferred to focus on the role which an international student organization could play in the sensitization of its constituents to the gender issue. However, we will take Wageningen Agricultural University in the Netherlands

- where the author is studying - as an example of a university which deals with the gender issue in its curriculum.

An introductory section will look at the status of women in agriculture in the world. Then I will give a short presentation of Wageningen Agricultural University in general, followed by a description of its "Department of Gender Issues in Agriculture".The role of students in ensuring that the gender issue is "on the agenda" will be discussed, and finally, I will outline the actions IAAS intends to take to address the topic "Women in Agriculture".

Women in Agriculture

In many countries, agricultural development means economic development. Changes in agriculture also have social implications. For many people all over the world, daily economic and social life is concentrated around, and dependent on, agricultural processes. Therefore, the role of women in agriculture has to be considered in this context.

Recognizing the substantial contribution of women is important for the development process. A paper from the Ministry of Foreign Affairs of the Netherlands[1] explicitly describes the role of women in agriculture in relation to development. I would like to mention some of the points raised here.

On a worldwide basis, women generate more than half the food that is produced and consumed in developing countries. Women are often the major and frequently the sole providers of the household food supply and other family welfare goods such as education and healthcare. Women are typically involved in post-harvest processing of food and non-food products. Women often trade self-produced agricultural products on a small scale and on informal markets. This production is the basis of livelihood for a majority of rural people.

Women's direct contribution to agricultural output is increasing: female labour input to family farms increases as cropping patterns shift to commercial food and non-food production. This can mean that obligations for women have become more burdensome, but that their legal status has not been upgraded accordingly. In many countries, women cannot become members of co-operatives or offical organizations for input supply or marketing, because they hold no registered title for land. When women are running cash enterprices, it is difficult for them to realize profits and make the best management decisions because they do not have independent access to credit and banking facilities.

The well known example of the experience of the milk co-operative movement in Gujarat and Andhra Pradesh in India illustrates how undervaluation of the contribution of women can lead to ineffective and inefficient situations :

> "In their initial form, the co-operatives were designed on the assumption that men own the cattle or buffalo, that they controlled family income and that they were the main decision makers in the dairy sector. It was typically overlooked that in reality it was women who did most of the milking and daily feeding and care, thus controlling certain aspects of the management. Consequently, when men were trained in improved feeding methods, better maintenance of hygiene or artificial insemination, this did not have the anticipated impact, because men did not have the animals constantly under their care and observation, as the women did. In addition, when men took the opportunity to obtain a higher cash income through milk sales, women found that they had less milk at their disposal for family consumption..."[2]

Project benefits often largely bypass women, and overall progress is often less than optimal because their potential is not fully utilized.

The role of women is often underestimated or neglected not only in developing countries, but also in industrialized countries. For a long time the farm women and their work have been "invisible" in research and policy. Farm women often do not have professional status and therefore enjoy less legal or social security. The income of a woman on a farm is often less then the income of her husband, even when both invest the same amount of time. It is also often very difficult for women with their own farm to be recognized and taken seriously as "women farmers" instead of being "just" a farmer's wife (which of course involves other tasks and responsibilities). Furthermore, women are still underrepresented in the traditionally male dominated agricultural organizations. A first step towards the improvement of the position of women is to make both women and men in the field, as well as in the policy making institutions, aware of their position.

From the above mentioned examples it is clear that paying attention to gender issues in the university curriculum is important. The students of today are the project leaders, development workers and policy-makers of tomorrow. To give an example of the way in which agricultural faculties deal with gender issues, I shall take a closer look at the Agricultural University of Wageningen in the Netherlands.

Wageningen Agricultural University

Since its foundation in 1918,Wageningen Agricultural University (known as WAU) is the only agricultural university or faculty in the Netherlands and has only one faculty: that of Agriculture and Environment. Apart from agriculture, research is undertaken in forestry, physical planning, biology, biotechnology, nutrition, food science, in environmental, economic and information fields and in the social sciences. Almost always this pertains to agricultural and environmental context. There are 60 different departments and 19 different degree programmes for the students to choose from. There are also 15 courses for students from abroad.

The university is highly international in orientation and has projects all over the world. Wageningen does a lot of research, and offers courses on tropical agriculture, tropical forestry and development studies as well. This tropical expertise results from the necessity in earlier years to train tropical agronomists for the agricultural systems in the former colonies, notably Indonesia and Suriname.

The University of Wageningen is aware of the importance of the social context of agriculture and there is a good representation of the "social" sciences: philosophy, rural development, sociology, extension science, law, history, public administration, and last but not least gender issues in agriculture. Several courses in those different disciplines are compulsory for each student and also for those who want to specialize in a more technical field. Students have the possibility of designing part of their curriculum themselves, and often they choose this kind of discipline to broaden their orientation.

Gender Studies at Wageningen[3]

Currently between 6 to 10 women are working at the department of Gender Issues in Agriculture, partly doing research, partly involved in education. The history of this department has not been without its struggles. In 1979 a special professor for Social Trends: Women's emancipation in Western and Non-Western Countries was appointed for half a day per week. In 1980 there was also a training position available for one teacher on gender issues. Emancipation Studies and gender issues finally merged in one department which is now known as the department for Gender Issues in Agriculture.[4] Students claim that the department would no longer exist, had it not been for their efforts to draw attention from the several university bodies to the educational and the social importance of having a focal point for Gender Issues.

The department deals with developing knowledge about and insight into the position of women, and the relations between women and men. Power plays an important role in gender issues. The department wants to show the inequality of power between women, and men and make a contribution towards a better balance in this respect via training and research. Very often the latter focus on the situation in the South. In the education process, there is emphasis on the importance of women's perception of events. Criticism of the educational system at the university from women students led to development of new methods in the department, which allow room for knowledge and questions from the students themselves. Students are being stimulated to take responsibility for their own education process.

The department offers several courses, some giving a broad overview, others more specialized. The introductory course "Gender Issues in Agriculture" gives students more insight into the way women and men are active in agriculture, and the crucial role of gender in this context. Other courses are: **Woman and Science, Research from a Gender Studies Perspective, Gender issues: theoretical approaches and strategies concerning gender issues in agricultural projects.** It also is possible to write a thesis on the topic Women in Agriculture. This specialized department is not the only one to offer courses on gender issues as these are also addressed elsewhere in the university. The department of Law offers courses on "Women, law and development in rural areas", while "Gender in tropical engineering" is available in the scientific domain.

So, gender issues receive considerable attention at Wageningen. However, there are a lot of students who have never had contact with the department dealing with gender issues or dealt with these in their courses. Introductory courses are only compulsory for the degree programmes on Tropical Land Use and Rural Development Studies. Though the other students can also choose the courses on gender issues in addition to their compulsory courses, there tends to be less and less time for such electives.

Most of the students taking the courses at the department are female. Of course this is quite logical and to be expected, but it would certainly do no harm for male students to get some insight into gender issues as well. This last point is more a problem of attitude, interest and motivation of the students themselves. Creating heightened awareness among the students still appears to be required.

Students and the Gender Dimension at Wageningen

At the end of the seventies, students played an important role in focusing attention on the gender dimension and forcing debate on this. As early as 1977 there was a "Boerinnengroep" - a farm women's group - at Wageningen. This is currently known as the "Working Group for Women in Agriculture" (WVL). The WVL is an example of an autonomous group of students who want to do something to correct the unequal power balance between women and men in agriculture. The WVL is independent of the university, in the sense that it is not bound to a department or degree programme.

The working group develops material for agricultural women and their organizations, and organizes courses to introduce students to the position of agricultural women in the Netherlands[5]. Every student can be active in the WVL, and certain activities can be part of a university study as the WVL permits students to write their thesis in the framework of a project from the WVL. Students can also be involved in the activities of WVL for a trial period. Both this and the thesis are acknowledged by the university as part of the curriculum of the students' degree programme. The working group tries to draw attention to the fact that greater attention should be given to women in agriculture throughout the research and teaching offered at the university.

Activities of this kind by student groups are very valuable and can be very effective because they generate practical results for women in agriculture, and create awareness among students. It is also good to see that the university reacts to such student activities in a positive way. This can be encouraging for IAAS members in other countries who want to start activities in the same direction.

The IAAS

The International Association of Agricultural Students,founded in 1957, brings together students from more than 40 countries all over the world. It is a wide network from local and national committees in member countries in Africa, Latin-America, Europe and the Asian Pacific region. The aims of the association are to encourage the exchange of ideas in all fields of agricultural education and practice, to promote international co-operation and understanding between students and to prepare the students for the problems they will have to deal with in their professional life as agronomists.

In each region, seminars are regularly organized as well as weeks concentrating on particular agricultural subjects - for example, a specific crop or farming system in the guest country, or on current international trends. These are open to students from all countries and are intended to foster the exchange of knowledge and experience between them. The social aspect is important as well. To get to know so many people from different cultures is an experience in itself. This dimension is even more emphasized during the so-called "exchange week", a bilateral event where groups of students from two countries visit each other.   The landscape, rural traditions and culture of the particular countries are studied during these periods.

The possibility of becoming acquainted with the daily life of a farmer in another country is offered by the IAAS Exchange Programme. Students can go for several months to a farm abroad and participate in its work. For many young people, this is the only practical experience they will get, as not all universities can put "hands-on experience" into the curriculum - though this is absolutely essential for someone who will be working as an agricultural professional.

At the annual IAAS World Congress, held each year in a different country, all national associations are able to meet. During the first week, the General Assembly is held, a meeting for discussions and actions on organization and structure. The other two weeks are dedicated to a special Congress Theme which is chosen by the guest country - "Youth, Environment and Development" (Brazil 1993), "Challenges of Marginal Areas" (Slovenia 1994), "Co-operatives, the Danish Way" (Denmark 1995) and "Tropical Agriculture" (Indonesia 1996).

Each year, every region has its own meeting as well. Structural and organizational aspects of the association are discussed and new projects are prepared. Again those meetings function as a way to get to know people from other cultures and backgrounds, to make international friendships, to have informal discussions about certain topics and to inform each other about the different ways the universities in the several countries design their courses. For many students it was during such an informal discussion that their eyes were opened to the fact that maybe the situation at the own university could be improved and that things could be organized differently.

In 1994 for the first time and with the help of a special working group, we launched the worldwide study of a specific theme. This topic was "Higher Agricultural Education" and it proved to be a "hot subject" in our co-operation with UNESCO and FAO. We wanted to give more structure to the informal discussions which were already taking place during the different meetings and to stimulate discussions at the universities in the home countries as well. At the General Assembly, we had a special one day forum on Higher Agricultural Education which included a discussion on the UNESCO Policy Paper "Change and

Development in Higher Education". This approach proved to be a great succes and appeared to respond to a real need. From the discussions, we found that the issue of "Women in Agriculture" was an important one for our students as well. Therefore we decided to have this as our topic for the coming year and at the same time remain active around the domain of higher education.

The higher education topic was a succesful one because students felt really involved. The same can be said for the theme "Women in Agriculture". From their own daily life, students feel that there is a difference in opportunities and power. This is not only true for countries in the South but also for those in the North. By way of example, in Ghana, almost all IAAS members are male. Women are absent because they are not in the the faculty and are few in the entire university. IAAS Ghana explains that in a poor family there is not enough money to let all children enter higher education. Preference is often given to allow the boys to study before the girls. In Austria, female students see their future as extension specialists in agriculture as very negative because they feel that very few farmers will take advice from a woman. They do not feel that they are taken seriously or fully respected. These kinds of experiences are very good to share with one other, especially since the agricultural faculties in a number of countries pay no attention to the gender issue at all.

In IAAS, it is satisfying to note that women are well represented. In some countries, they reflect the overall enrolment of female students at the home institutions. More often the amount of women in IAAS is even greater than could be expected given the ratio of female to male students at the universities. Women are very well represented on the boards and leading bodies of the IAAS and in the last few years, there have always been women on the Executive Committee. This is the international board of IAAS, chosen each year at the General Assembly. It has a President, Vice-President and Secretary-General. In 1994-1995, all three of these officers were women - a situation which has been repeated in 1995-96.

IAAS Activities and Potential in relation to Gender Issues

A student organization like the IAAS can be an excellent conduit for sensitizing students to the gender issue. Several actions can stimulate them to look around in the agricultural reality of the own country and take a closer look to the attention which is given to gender issues in the university curriculum. In particular, because an international organization like IAAS also gives an opportunity to exchange experiences with students from other countries, students can more easily evaluate the situation in their own country. Thus, they can be inspired to have discussions about the curriculum with university staff, or integrate practical ideas in a new project.

When dealing with the topic of "Women in agriculture" we have the following objectives:
* to promote the interchange of ideas and to create awareness among agricultural students of the situation of women in agriculture in the various countries and regions;
* to stimulate discussion among agricultural students and at the universities on the gender issue in this domain.

A special working group is co-ordinating the activities in the different countries. In several countries field studies will be carried out, and each country can organize one-day excursion to interview women farmers and gather information. This field work is not meant to yield sophisticated research studies, but should function as a starting point for discussion. During regional meetings there will be an evaluation of these field studies, and countries can inform each other about their different experiences. In the following months, the national and local committees can organize seminars and discussion groups at their universities. At the World Congress in 1996 in Indonesia, a special forum on "Women in Agriculture" will be held to present the results of these different surveys.

Actions will be varied. For instance, local committees will be encouraged to contact local organizations outside IAAS to work together on the topic. In the Netherlands, there could be contact with the earlier mentioned WVL (Working group Women in Agriculture) which could be of help by providing expertise in the field and information material. A specially developed role-playing exercise by the WVL has also examined the position of women on family farms, a project which has interesting transfer possibilities for use by IAAS. This strategy could be used by an IAAS team in other countries. The prime purpose of this approach is to encourage farm women themselves to acquire a better insight into their social and professional role. At the same time, the game could be a very practical and informal way for the students to make actual contact with farm women in order to develop a better understanding of their problems. This is a concrete approach and one which could interest students in different socio-cultural contexts where attitudes to women and their conditions are extremely varied. Moreover, this is a good example of learning by experience.

For several years, IAAS has had a special development programme, called "the Village Concept Project" (VCP). This means that local and foreign students in Agronomy and Medicine work together with the inhabitants in a village for the improvement of infrastructure, agriculture and hygiene. For the students, this activity is partly a learning process, partly the offer of assistance. In these projects there could be more attention paid to the gender dimension. In the framework of the topic "Women in Agriculture", the role of women could be analysed more explicitly by the students and discussed with all people who are involved.

Conclusion: towards Equality, Development and Peace

Through its actions, and not necessarily on a large-scale, IAAS could increase awareness, among students and in the field, to questions of *equality* of women and men, both at the universities and in the agricultural domain. We have seen that agriculture plays a key role in the *development* process and the huge role women play in this process. Recognizing this role and using women's potential is crucial to be able to let the development process proceed effectively and optimally. It is very important that agricultural graduates realize this during their studies. Activities from IAAS and other student organizations could play a role here. As students have the right to be critical of quality and relevance of their courses, they should be involved in the design of the curriculum. Inspired by discussions and experiences with their counterparts from other countries, they could make proposals for more attention to gender issues in their own curriculum. Finally, both female and male students working together in activities where gender is a factor can make a contribution to achieving the ultimate goal of a conflict-free society. Being an international organization IAAS is well equipped to contribute to understanding and co-operation between students all over the world. In this regard, the ability of its members to influence future social policy-making is considerable and must be strongly encouraged.

Acknowledgements

The author wishes to thank *Mirjam Troost*, former President of IAAS, who took the initiative for this article; *Corine van Reeuwijk* from WVL for providing information about the activities of the working group; and the *Department for Gender Issues in Agriculture,* Wageningen Agricultural University for providing information about the department.

Notes

1. *Women and Agriculture.* Sector Paper Women and Development no 1, Directorate General for International Cooperation, Ministry of Foreign Affairs, The Netherlands, 1989.

2. Ibid. p. 9.

3. Information about the history of the and the offered courses I obtained from the *Studiegids Vrouwenstudies in the Landbouw, 1994-1995.*

4. Probably there will be a merger with the Department of Sociology.

5. See the information leaflet *"Werkgroep Vrouwen in de Landbouw"* A publication of WVL.

Peace Studies

Sanàa W. Osseiran

International Peace Research Association

Introduction

Linking equality, democracy and peace with gender issues is a recent phenomenon that was adopted unanimously in Nairobi in 1985 in the Forward Looking Strategies for the Advancement of Women to the Year 2000 (the FLS). It should be noted that the first international conference on women, held in Mexico in 1975 started looking into this linkage but it took one decade more to have it adopted as a comprehensive strategy.

Indeed, this coincided with peace research and peace studies being incorporated at the university level in several universities in the West mainly in North America, Canada and in the Nordic countries. Similarly, the contributions of numerous women peace researchers in the International Peace Research Association (IPRA) increased the number of its female members who understood the existing links between development, human rights and democracy. Thus, it is not surprising to find that one of IPRA's eighteen commissions is on Women and Peace which has always assured the linkage between these two entities.

This international sensitization to the connection between gender studies and the ideals of equality, democracy and peace came at a time when the Arab World was immersed in many interstate conflicts - Israel/Palestine/Arab states, Iran/Iraq war, the Gulf war and intrastate conflicts in Lebanon, Algeria, Sudan, Yemen, the Iraq/Kurdish conflict and other internal conflicts involving Islamic movements. Therefore, the general environment in the Arab region during the past twenty years has been geared towards a culture of war in which women's issues on the whole were not a priority.

Moreover, most of the countries in the Arab World profess in their constitution to be Islamic countries and consequently follow the family status law with regard to women's rights. However, it should be pointed out that according to some Arab Muslim women who have worked on these issues, Islamic jurisprudence has not developed since the fifteenth century and has not followed what the Quran stipulates about the need to change in accordance with the needs, and development of Muslim societies. Those Arab women who are aware of their rights, whether they are Muslims or Christians, find state legislation discriminatory towards their sex. For example only 8 out of 21 Arab countries have signed the United Nations Convention on the Elimination of all Forms of Discriminations Against Women, and Lebanon is not amongst these. Consequently, the need to have national laws reaffirming or consistent with international standards is an ongoing challenge for women in the Arab World.

The cultural environment in the Arab World has taken a step forward in women's education and employment. Nevertheless, 62% of the illiterate population are women in the Arab World. Indeed, literacy education programmes seem to be a priority for women who are actively working either in higher education or in non-governmental organizations. Governments have also given women's education greater priority and admit the need to democratize education, to include democracy in education and to incorporate human rights and peace education. These priorities are a result of the Conference of Arab Ministers of Education which met for the first time in 17 years in Cairo in June1994. Therefore, awareness on these issues is currently acknowledged.

This chapter will deal with the case of higher education in Lebanon where the 17-year war had a devastating impact on higher education. It necessitated the creation of branches for many universities outside of Beirut. This has been the case for the Lebanese and the Saint Joseph Universities and has had a positive as well as a negative impact. On the positive side, university studies were accessible to more people who could not afford to study in the capital, and has led to the creation of eight new institutions of higher education. Conversely, it increased the division in communal affiliation where the hostilities forced religious groups to live in ghettos. Furthermore, the number of foreign students and exchanges shrank tremendously, and contact with the outside world became impossible.

The Lebanese Context

According to a UNESCO fact finding mission in 1991 priorities in higher education include staff development, the expansion of science and technology, including equipment and materials, and the need to establish contact with the academic world abroad. A recent report prepared for the United Nations Development Programme recommended the strengthening of democratic practices, enhancing the sense of national identity and social responsibility, and increasing awareness of human rights through text books and other teaching materials, the development of civic and human rights programmes both in schools and in society, and eliminating the extensive gender bias in the Lebanese school system.

The awareness of the link between development and equity as well as the place of Arab women in decision-making began more than twenty years ago in Lebanon. The establishment of the Institute on Women's Studies as part of the Lebanese American University (formerly the Beirut College for Women) in 1973 is an example. This Institute has always played a key role in furthering awareness of women's perspectives, rights, education, and their role in promoting peace and human rights within Lebanese society and in the Arab World in general. To this end, it publishes a quarterly journal on women's issues, as well as books and research on various themes touching on women's development. The Institute which is part of the Lebanese American University, has recognized that its priority is work on children in conflict situations based on promoting values of tolerance, of rights and respect for others, as well as their own rights. The long war has made teachers aware that human rights, peace education and democracy have to be taught to children, as they will represent the hope for the future generation and, so, for the country. In addition, one of the activities of the Institute has been its social literacy programme for women. This programme focuses on women's awareness of their legal rights, environment, health and family education. A curricula has been developed by the Institute for this purpose and has been used in several Arab countries such as Egypt, Tunisia, Algeria, Jordan and Yemen. Saint Joseph University in Lebanon is teaching this course to social workers.

The Institute has contributed to linking the issue of development with employment. To this end, they are undertaking research projects that focus on the link between employed women and decision-making within the family. Moreover, the Lebanese American University offers five courses related to women, such as their economy, the sociology of Arab women, women in literature and the media and the psychology, of women.

All female professors interviewed underlined that they do try to bring out women's issues, perspectives and rights indirectly in their Humanities and Social Science courses. Nevertheless, there was unanimity in their replies that specific courses in the curriculum do not exist because they felt that neither the students nor the country are ready for it. Therefore, all the courses on women at the Lebanese American University have been elective courses and have drawn very small attendance from students. There are several reasons for such low attendance. First they do not help the students to find employment after graduation. Second, the cultural environment is not encouraging. As one student related to her professor "it is better not to be aware of our rights since the environment is not yet ready to acknowledge them." Third, there is a lethargic attitude on the part of female students regarding their perception of how they, themselves, can really contribute to change in their society. As a result, awareness of their role, and confidence in their ability to change has to be increased.

Universities in Lebanon give great freedom to their professors in making their own decisions. The university management does not interfere in the choice of elective courses and academic freedom is well respected. Yet, the university has not played its role as the leader in sensitizing students - both male and female alike. While some female professors have kept their male colleagues informed about their research activities on women's issues, others have remained indifferent to the whole question of women and their rights in a democratic society. Therefore, one can summarize the attitude of most universities in Lebanon as being neutral towards gender issues in the curriculum. This raises the question as to the role the universities in Lebanon have played in promoting peace and linking human resource development to democracy and human rights teaching.

All professors interviewed stressed that the universities in the past did not link education to employment in general. The link between higher education and manpower has never been on the agenda of universities. Education has to serve society's needs by monitoring changes in its structure and the effect of these on the development process. This linkage has bearing on human rights, equity and democracy because such education enhances the perception of how poverty, unemployment and other marginalized sectors of society can be causes of unrest and violence.

Some female professors considered that the word "gender" is Western in origin and needs to be arabized in content and in language. Indeed, some pointed out that democracy and peace are used incorrectly. None of them contested the importance of teaching gender issues or of linking these to human rights, democracy and peace. Yet, none has had the time or the funds to do sufficient research on these themes. Most have worked on the legal aspects with regard to discrimination against women.

In 1995, one professor introduced a course on feminism focusing on the history of theories from the 18th century onward. This course permitted students to select themes concerning women in the Arab world. Others have stated that they address gender issues in their Humanities programmes. However, the question of gender remains non-existent in the Arab world, and its development is hindered by an absence of legal thinking on the subject.

Is this unawareness due to the fact that universities have never attempted to introduce such themes in their curriculum? One's answer is inclined to be affirmative, since, as mentioned by those surveyed, academic freedom in Lebanon is highly respected, and university management does not interfere with its professors in the selection of courses. On the contrary, the example of the Lebanese American University is positive since five courses relevant to women have been introduced, including one on peace and conflict resolution.

Many respondents pointed out the need to work on teaching methodology and to sensitize teachers themselves regarding the links between peace and gender issues. As one professor at the Saint Joseph University, Teacher's Training Institute in Education observed:

"It is essential to train teachers to follow a reflective teaching methodology. While generally non-existent, the Saint Joseph University has launched a course in reflective educational methodology in an effort to contribute to the rehabilitation of the teaching profession. Teachers should emphasize that there is not one single answer, strategy, or type of questioning. Rather, there are a multiplicity of approaches and views with regard to each problem. This, in itself, enhances democratic values and promotes civic education. Hence, it is vital to have education which is related to and has an impact on civic life and on social development. In addition, giving students the right to

express their opinions, to develop their own understanding
of the terms they use and to share these with fellow students,
will permit them to open their minds to the complexity of
issues at hand and their interdependence."

A good number agreed that democracy permits creativity.
Questioning permits university students to develop the analytical
capacity necessary to reflect on what is happening in their
immediate environment - whether this be the family, society at
large or the university.

Given the need to increase awareness, what would or should be
the role of higher education in this field? Almost all professors
underlined the need to introduce courses on human rights, peace
and democracy not only at university level, but also in
elementary schools. Some favoured introducing these as separate
courses, while others thought that they should be slowly
introduced through the Social Sciences, Law, International
Relations, Political Sciences, Literature and the Humanities. One
professor felt that a course on Development - and in particular a
university chair in this field - would highlight the linkage
between this process and human rights and peace. Others noted
that a chair in Human Rights and Democracy could raise
consciousness and have a multiplier effect.

It may be noted the International Peace Research Association
(IPRA), in co-operation with UNESCO and Lebanese educators
produced a Handbook for Teaching and Resource Material in
Conflict Resolution, *Education for Human Rights, Peace and
Democracy* in July 1994. This addressed intermediate and
secondary school teachers and will be piloted in 30 Lebanese
schools with a view to incorporating it into the curriculum. There
are, therefore, indications that peace education, human rights and
democracy are starting to be introduced through the educational
system.

In general, therefore, teachers agreed on the need to change teaching methodology and to raise student awareness at all levels of formal and non-formal education.

Moreover, the role of Lebanese non-governmental organizations should not be forgotten as these were the first to link the issue of development with human rights and democracy. The Lebanese Association for Human Rights (ALDHOM) gives many courses every year on different aspects of human rights, including gender issues. The Lebanese Association of Women Researchers is also beginning to work in this area.

Strategies for Change

In order to determine approaches which could enhance the conceptualization and teaching of Peace Studies in the Lebanese university curriculum, the survey conducted sought to ascertain:

- Whether gender issues permeated teaching and research work and the kind of feedback received;
- How and to what extent professorial input to the decision-making process concerning the university curricula, faculty policies and university management has changed over the past ten years;
- Whether equality, democracy and peace are priority issues for academics in terms of improving human resource development and whether other issues should also be incorporated in the curriculum. In addition, respondents were asked to describe the support received and obstacles encountered;
- Whether themes related to peace could be indirectly included in the courses taught and which were most likely to sensitize students to important aspects;
- To what extent normative instruments such as international conventions and recommendations regarding higher education, peace, discrimination against women and

participatory democracy were debated in society, amongst faculty, at the management level, and between male and female professors;

- Whether teaching human rights as a separate course is more conducive to an understanding and development of peace-related themes, or whether this should be integrated in all Social and Political Science courses dealing with the governance and management of society;
- Reactions - as professors, women, citizens, wives and mothers - to the dichotomy between the increase in women's illiteracy, poverty, as well as in the economic crisis of a post-conflict society and the aims of human resource development;
- Affiliation to international NGOs specialized in higher education and women, and the effectiveness of these bodies in raising awareness of the gender dimension of peace;
- The reasons why the specific contribution of women to the peace process has not had the success expected. This also sought to identify constraints and to understand women's definitions of and attitudes to peace, democracy and equality since these need to be seen against the Arab culture;
- How the professoriate has contributed in an innovative manner to defining the new vision of Arab women which is required if their role in the peace process is to be fully realized.

As a result of these interviews, it was suggested that change could be effected in various ways - some of which are not without difficulties:

- So far, the incorporation of gender issues at the university level has resulted from the individual efforts of female professors. This has been a very small step. Nevertheless, with the relative peace in Lebanon, more courses can now focus on promoting women's vision of their society so as to prepare a new generation who can play a more effective role in its future development. The peace process in the region will permit educational innovation so that conflict prevention and resolution might be incorporated into the teaching content. This should address issues related to both civil and international mediation.

- It is evident that organizations active in higher education renewal can play a fundamental role in this undertaking. The UNESCO Chair Programme, which has already initiated a number of international teaching and research projects related to human rights and development, would be one useful instrument to raise consciousness both amongst the teaching corps and the students.

- International non-governmental organizations such as the International Federation of University Women could seek new members amongst female professors in Lebanon. Since these academics have led an active sensitization campaign which has continued despite the very difficult conditions of the war, they would benefit from the possibilities offered by NGOs to linking international development with local issues.

- Research grants for advanced female students who are studying development, peace and gender issues are an essential mechanism. The International Peace Research Association offers this sort of assistance and other international non-governmental institutions can follow this example since the need is great.

- In this respect, the major regional NGO, the Association of Arab Universities can urge its member institutions to introduce gender issues in university curriculum and to devote serious attention to peace research. This field is both rich and complex as it clearly has to include issues related to equity, academic freedom, human rights and the exercise of democracy.

- Arab women researchers should do further work to alter the stereotyping of women in textbooks and in academic literature. This is a very urgent problem which results in serious discriminatory practices against women. It is thus vital that children develop positive and equitable attitudes with regard to the social roles and potential of women.

- As the forum which prepares tomorrow's leaders, the university should include a gender dimension in its teaching and research programmes.
- Contemporary Lebanese writers have written extensively on themes related to war and peace. The university can indeed promote more research in gender issues from within the literary culture by questioning and introducing new visions and methodology based on different interpretations. The university should work on highlighting the interdependence of civilizations and of ideas to illustrate how they can influence each other in a positive way. To do this, the teaching corps has to discuss these issues and agree on their common objectives. Otherwise, awareness is purely individual and has limited impact.

The importance of this aspect cannot be underestimated. After all, what is the purpose of a university education, if students' vision is not broadened so that they can understand how they might best contribute to the advancement of their society? One female professor claimed that she was more hopeful in the sixties because of the dynamism of the social debate led by academics and others at that time. Today in the nineties, there seems to be more fanaticism, as well as a ghetto mentality and serious social dislocation. Such a statement should be sufficient to galvanize universities to meet the challenges of higher education in the 21st century - with education for tolerance and human rights being included at the university level. Another subject for inclusion in university courses is the economic power of women. Since poor and illiterate women become more independent when they work and earn their own living, it is important that this factor is widely known and its implications understood.

- All professors agreed that the social level - rather than the curriculum - is the real cause of many problems. Hence the impact of communication technology, and of course the media, must be taken into account during the educational process.

- Conceptualization of key issues from within the Lebanese and Arab culture can commence at the university level because, here, it is possible to link the level of a society's development with developmental theory. Social philosophy can be developed to incorporate gender issues via respect for the right to dignity of each human being. Correct attitudes, thinking and behaviour are indispensable for the proper development of any human society. Gender issues can be incorporated into this approach.

- Courses in Development Studies can, as a first step, provide the necessary interdisciplinary approach to gender issues - as well as to equality, democracy and peace because they reflect on the specific problems of Lebanese and Arab society and the best solutions for these. The teaching of such courses requires expert knowledge of the culture of development which combines, as one professor highlighted, the issues, respect for oneself and for others and a methodology to understand this process and its various components.

- The entire question of peace remains an extremely sensitive subject for the female professors interviewed. On the one hand, they stressed the importance of Peace Studies to serve the aim of peace-building. On the other hand, some felt that there is ambiguity with regard to the legitimacy of the issue itself in any country where conflict remains unresolved or where sovereignty is not respected. In such situations, peace and war issues cannot be totally separated. Even promoting the concept of peace might possibly be considered as a type of surrender. Hence, for any university intending to set up a course, Peace Studies can be an extremely delicate area, and, as a curriculum component, might be more relevant to international relations than to social development. Above all, tolerance is constantly required to deal with the inevitable paradoxes inherent in the theme and to ensure that objectivity is preserved. Yet, despite the difficulties, it was felt that Peace Studies, as a university course, can provide the essential basis for linking education with development, equity and the promotion of human rights. Ultimately, peace results from a comprehensive outlook linking all relevant issues of which gender is an integral part. So, given its educational potential, Peace Studies merit serious consideration.

Conclusion

Over the years, Lebanese women have certainly tried to contribute to peace in their society. But, as in most conflict-ridden countries, their priority has been to protect their immediate families and to assist those directly affected by the war.

The years of war have also damaged universities in Lebanon which have suffered from being isolated from the outside world during this period. Nevertheless, it is now that they need support to undertake research and to establish strategies to help promote national development and the gender dimension of this process.

The field of higher education can incorporate and promote these issues through international co-operation projects which sponsor training and research. It may take a decade or two to see real results in Lebanon, but, ultimately, not only the country but the entire region can benefit from these initiatives.

Intergovernmental organizations and NGOs can help enhance the link between regional and international development trends. However, the new development models cannot be external - to be durable, they should be articulated from within and it is important that issues such as equality, democracy, peace and gender be seen in light of the needs of the region.

With regard to the gender dimension, the 4th World International Conference on Women (Beijing, 1995) should be considered as a positive initiative on the part of the United Nations as it permitted Arab women to meet one another and thus to exchange concerns and interests. Such conferences are important, but debate alone is not sufficient. Rather they should serve to generate regional encounters which can identify and monitor priority action to be undertaken in each area of the development process. This chapter has sought to emphasize that education in the Arab world must privilege teacher training as the prime vehicle for ensuring that those priority concepts related to peace - which clearly must include gender - are appropriately covered.

Bibliography

Books:

Moghaizel, Laure. *Your Employment Rights: A Legal Guide*, Lebanese Association for Human Rights, Catholic Publication, Araya, 1994.

Moghaizel, Laure. *Women in Lebanese Legislation: In light of International Conventions and in Comparison with Arab Legislation*, Institute of Women's Studies in the Arab World, Beirut University College, Beirut, 1985.

Sharoni, Simona. *Gender and the Israeli-Palestinian Conflict: The Politics of Women's Resistance*, Syracuse University Press, 1995.

Pietila, Hilkka & Vickers, Jeanne. "Equality, Development & Peace" in *The Future of the United Nations System* to be published by Mershan Center, Ohio University, September 1995.

Reports:

Al-Hibri, Aziza. "An Analytical Research Project on Family Status Laws in a Selected Number of Arab Countries", E/ESCWA/SD/1994/WG-3-WO-/8, Amman, September 1994.

Krayam, Hassan & Titsworth, Jack. *State, Society, Sustainable Human Development & Support for Good Governance in Lebanon*, Draft Report for UNDP, Beirut, April-May 1995.

The Role of Women In the Non-Violent Conduct: The Palestinian-Israeli Conflict. Dossier no. 3, published by the International University of People's Institutions for Peace, Rovereto, August to September 1994.

Les droits des femmes au Liban: situation & perspective dans le cadre de la construction national, UNESCO, SHS, mars 1993.

Needs Assessment Mission in the Fields of Education & Cultural Heritage, (Lebanon), UNESCO publication, May 1991.

International Conference on Education, UNESCO, Geneva 3 to 8 October 1994.

Report on the Regional Arab Meeting for the Preparation of the 4th International Conference on Women, Beijing 1995, 6 to 10 November, ESCWA Publication, Amman 1994.

Report on Fifth Conference of Ministers of Education & Those Responsible for Economic Planning in the Arab States, UNESCO, June 1994.

Draft Regional Plan of Action for the Advancement of Arab Women to the Year 2005, ESCWA Publication, no. ESCWA/SD/1994/WG-3-WOM/ 4O October 1994.

Evaluation and Exposé Report on the Development Achievements of Arab Women since the Nairobi International Conference, ESCWA/SD/1994/WG.3-WOM/3, October 1994.

Kallab-Bissat, Ilham. *Observations on Paper Dealing With Women & Peace in the Arab Region*, ESCWA Publication, number E/ESCWA/SD/1994/WG.3-WOM/5/Add2., 6 to 10 November, Amman 1994.

Moghaizel, Laure. "The Role of Women in Peace and Conflict Resolution in Lebanon," in IPRA/International Alert report on *Conflict Resolution Training Workshop*, Jal El-Deeb, UNESCO/Paris, December 1994.

Sfeir, Salma. The Role of Women in Political Parties in Lebanon, in IPRA/International Alert report on Conflict Resolution Training Workshop, Jal El-Deeb, UNESCO/Paris, December 1994.

Interviews:

Dr. Abou Nasser, Julinda, Head of Institute on Women's Studies in the Arab World, Lebanese American University, Beirut, 10 August 1995.
Dr. Amiyuni Takiedine, Mona, American University of Beirut (AUB), Civilization Sequence Programme, Beirut, August 1995.

Dr. Charafidine, Fahmia, Lebanese University, Institute of Social Sciences, Beirut, 8 August 1995.

Dr. Kallab-Bissat, Ilham, Lebanese University, Faculty of Fine Arts, 10 August 1995.

Dr. Khalaf, Mona, Lebanese American University, Business School, Beirut, 8 August 1995.

Dr. Moghaizel- Nasr, Nada, St. Joseph University, Teacher's Training Institute, Beirut, 9 August 1995.

Dr. Shehadeh Rustum, Lamia, Associate Professor, American University of Beirut (AUB), Former Head of Civilization Sequence Programme, Mansourieh, 10 August 1995.

Teacher Training and the Promotion of Gender Equality: A Case Study of Israeli Society

Rina Shachar
Bar-Ilan University, Israel

Introduction

The higher education system in Israel has been revolutionized in recent years. While in the past, there were only 5 Israeli Universities and a limited number of colleges in Israel, over the last 2 years, a rapid development has occurred and new colleges opened, both in and outside the cities, so that high school graduates' access to higher education has been facilitated. This is one of the techniques that the government is employing to prevent a "brain drain" from the country. In addition, this greater openness to higher education that the government is developing, conforms to the declared democratic aspirations of Israel. The primary aim of higher education is to train more and more experts in different areas to advance society and the quality of life. Furthermore, as Israel is a central pool of technology, research and development in the Middle East, both the Arabs and Jews in Israel have much to gain from this new openness. The changes that Israel is going through in preparation for the peace process and increased democratization, in relations with the Arabs as well, creates advancement opportunities for both Jewish and Arab Israeli women. Today, women are in the process of entering key executive positions, and the options for women are more open in different areas such as Medicine, Law and Communications. In higher education, we see many changes - for instance, there are more female students than males in undergraduate programmes. The figures for 1992 attested to 54.3% female students in Israel, which is a greater percentage than in the United States, Japan, England and Sweden. In Master's programmes, women made up 50.6% of students, which seems to be a ratio of 1:1. However, in doctoral programmes, women (42.4%) continue to be fewer than men. Also, in spite of the massive entry of women into the various academic programmes, we still see a significantly larger proportion of men in comparison to women who graduate with degrees in Science and Technology.

Table 1:
Distribution of Students According to Sex - Summarized Data of all of the Universities in Israel in 1993

Area	Economics		Law		Computers	
Degree	Men	Women	Men	Women	Men	Women
Undergraduate	66%	34%	54%	46%	72%	28%
Graduate	73%	27%	57%	43%	76%	24%
Doctorate	82%	18%	70%	30%	76%	24%

The implications of the above illustrated division[1] between men and women in the different areas of higher education are expressed in the descriptive data of the Israeli work market, where most of the more rewarding positions are occupied by men. This situation further emphasizes the importance of higher education for women as it allows greater mobility and easier access to higher level positions in the Israeli work force. Moreover, one can clearly see that there is a direct correlation between the higher education of women and work; 74% of women with higher education qualifications are employed, although today women represent only 45% of the work force in the country.

Findings from various studies show, however, that in order for a woman to hold a position similar to that of a man, she needs to have a higher level of education - in the Public Service, the average is 2 years more education.

In spite of the educational requirements demanded of women, the salary gap averages approximately 30-35%, in favour of men (Ephroni, 1990). A similar picture is seen in the political system, where the political profiles of women in local municipalities show that they were always more educated than their male counterparts. This means that higher education is a very important tool and resource for women in their advancement into prestigious positions in work as well as in politics (Herzog, 1994).

Gender Inequality within the Educational System

Israel has always expressed the slogan of social equality. Nevertheless, in reality, gender inequality is obvious throughout all of the social sectors: in high-level positions in the economy, in the professional sector, in politics, in the armed forces and in the media. Moreover, this inequality is expressed in the observable lack of women in the executive administrative levels of most organizational hierarchies.

This is the context in which the processes of socialization, starting from toddlers to adolescence, occurs (Shachar, 1993). One may ask the question: What is the role of the educational system, which is a central agent of socialization, in the perpetuation of the existing situation? An analysis of various studies on the Israeli educational system over the last decade can provide an answer.

Safir (1986) presents data from a large number of researchers who claim that the "cultivating environment" is of significant influence in the increasing differences between boys and girls in Israel in the various cognitive areas. According to Safir, the older one becomes, the greater the gap between the sexes in all of the areas studied, to the disadvantage of the girls. Safir further indicates that the gaps increase within the educational system itself, and brings forth findings from Lieblich's (1985) study which included 2,700 Jewish and Arab children in a representative national sample. The findings make it clear that at the age of six there are no differences between the sexes on the

Wechsler Intelligence Tests (WPSSI). This means that the entrance to school is on an equal basis on the cognitive level. However, at the age of nine, Jewish boys begin to show greater performance compared to girls in the verbal subtests. At age thirteen, boys' performance on the IQ tests are significantly higher than girls, while at age sixteen, the accumulation of points on the IQ shows a 12 point advantage in favour of the boys. A very similar picture is seen in the Arab sector so one cannot claim that the Jewish population is in a better position than the Arabs with regard to gender equality.

The research findings among gifted children also indicate a discouraging picture. Safir presented earlier data indicating the difficulties that gifted girls have, and the fact that their numbers decrease with age. Although the number of gifted boys and girls are about the same at younger ages, there is no tendency among parents to cultivate and invest time and resources in their daughters as they will "find it harder later to get a husband".

Gifted teenage girls do claim, however, that it is harder for them in classes with gifted boys because they are few in number and are treated in a patronising manner. Moreover, according to teachers' reports, these girls also encounter problems outside the classroom as they find it hard to create social relationships with boys who feel threatened by them.

The latest findings of the Department of Education (1992) indicate that the composition of the classrooms in relation to gifted children is a ratio of 1:3 girls and 2:3 boys at a younger age. In later years, the number of girls decreases significantly, and this is without any relation to the higher levels of intelligence among girls. It must be noted that when comparisons are made between those in Israel and the United States, the gap in cognitive performance between the sexes appears at an earlier age in Israel than in the U.S. (Safir, 1986).

The Causes of Gender Inequality

Given the above evidence, one must ask: why does the educational system in Israeli society seem to cultivate inequality? Researchers are certain that one of the more important reasons explaining the gaps between sexes is the teachers' stereotyped attitudes towards the girls and boys in the classrooms. These can be described as sexist attitudes, although the teachers themselves are usually not aware of such reactions (Ben Zvi-Mayer, Hertz-Lazarovitz and Safir, 1990). Furthermore, these attitudes are prevalent amongst more as well as less experienced teachers of both sexes.

In a later study, researchers claimed that the children, like the teachers, perceive boys as more talented in most of the areas checked, while the picture becomes more serious as age increases (Safir, Herz-Lazarovitz, Ben-Zvi-Mayer and Kupermintz 1992).

There is no doubt that the system's low expectations of girls is a self-fulfilling prophecy, and cultivates low self-esteem and distrust in their abilities. According to researchers, it is possible that the children in classrooms unconsciously internalize an adult world characterized by stereotypes, which are reinforced by teachers' attitudes and latent messages.

Additional evidence may be found in Abrahami-Einat's work (1993) which checked latent and overt messages in the educational system. In her work, evidence is also found to reflect stereotyped attitudes of teachers towards both sexes as well as their low expectations of girls in comparison to those of boys. An analysis of teachers' comments on the report cards of boys and girls in junior high schools shows that boys were given very specific advice such as: "your achievements have been excellent in the following subjects a., b., and c. and you have to work on subjects e., f., and g". The comments were clear, definitive and consistent regarding most of the boys' report cards. Among girls, however, quite a different type of comment was made pertaining to their good behaviour, social skills, co-operative attitudes or attractive handwriting. From this study it may be seen that teachers, in a latent way, direct boys to instrumental tasks or roles, whereas the girls are directed towards more expressive roles or occupations in society.

The Effects of Gender Inequality on Achievements and Aspirations

Amit and Moshevitz-Hadar (1989) compare the achievements of girls and boys in Mathematics in high school and the relation between these achievements and causal attributions of success or failure. Their study indicated the existence of a very well known picture, which is nothing less than a natural acceleration of the situation in the elementary schools. Boys outnumber girls by 2:1 in 5 point Maths which is the top level of the subject in high-school, although the latter group's achievements are equal or above those of the boys. One may conclude from this that the more prestigious courses, which may be viewed as important stepping stones into highly rewarding jobs in the labour market, as well as entry into academic and professional life, have become less accessible for girls. The study's findings show that the boys and girls have opposite attitudes towards success or failure and that these differences are particularly salient among those students who are high achievers. Boys regard their success as being due to their personal ability, whereas able girls tend to attribute their good results to external and random factors.

An overall picture of this research indicates that the problem in Mathematics is growing within the educational system. The main problems are:

1.   low levels of achievement among girls in Mathematics in elementary school;
2.   lower coverage of high school Mathematics material amongst girls;

3. lower levels of achievement among girls who take Science subjects to enter university. This results from their limited previous experience in comparisonto boys.

There is no doubt that girls do not realize their full potential. Consequently, many fail to explore or develop their own capacities either during their education or once they enter the work force. This partially explains why young women do not enter or rise in highly rewarding and prestigious professions such as Engineering, Informatics, Economics and R and D fields.

Ayalon (1988) claims that even at the age of 17 girls and boys express their vocational aspirations very differently . Boys aspire to professions with higher economic rewards than their level of education would permit, whereas girls seem content to take lower paid jobs although their education would allow them to aim much higher. Here, one can clearly see gender differentiation, as well as where this will lead in a number of years within the work force.

If, in addition to the above, we add the textbooks which encompass overt and latent stereotyped messages (Maller, 1991), the media which reinforces the stereotypes and returns women to their traditional roles (Lemish and Tidhar, 1990), as well as parental and teachers' attitudes to and expectations for boys and girls (Safir, 1986), we receive a very gloomy picture, in which most of the socialization agents, crowned by the educational system, perpetuate the inequality between the sexes. The picture described above reflects the existing situation in Western society. Evidence can be found for solving the problem of gender inequality: AAUW Report (1992). Baker, (1986); Lee, (1991); Sadker & Sadker (1985); State of Michigan, Department of Education, Office of Sex Equity in Education (June, 1990).

Solving the Problem of Gender Inequality

The socialization process is a long one which continues within the system for approximately 18 years, and is mainly carried out by women (kindergarten teachers, teachers, counsellors, supervisors and principals). One could say that women within the educational system "duplicate" themselves and their attitudes - both consciously and unconsciously - and thus create further generations of boys and girls with stereotyped gender attitudes.

The strategies for change must therefore be applied by the young teacher trainees within the colleges and universities, and among the more experienced teachers, principals and other educational personnel. Furthermore, all of the components of the system should be incorporated: study programmes, seminars, textbooks, teaching methods and the media. Different intervention programmes exist and have even been shown to be successful, However, over time, they have not been allocated the necessary support and resources from the Ministry of Education (Ben Zvi-Mayer and Shamai, unpublished; Zidman, Walker and Rom, 1992).

Ben Zvi-Mayer and Shamai's Intervention Programme, which was employed among elementary school children, was successful in decreasing the sexual status of various occupations, while promoting an equal image of characteristic traits. Moreover, among girls, the changes were much more significant than among boys. This programme, whose goal was to increase the number of female students in high school Science courses, showed that female students with potential can in fact be located, cultivated and influenced in their choice of courses, such as choosing 5-point Mathematics. Furthermore, this Intervention Programme which included an accompanying support system, was shown to significantly increase the number of girls who successfully finished this stage of their education. It thus represents the gateway to higher education in Engineering or the exact

Sciences, while being integrated into the system of research and development.

Hertz-Lazarovitz's work (1988, 1990), as well as the studies of other researchers (Herz-Lazarovitz and Shadell, 1992; Chasidov, 1994) indicate that the creation of an "alternative" study environment encourages gender equality and dramatically increases the achievements of girls. Here, an additional question may be asked: why is it that intervention programmes which were shown to be successful in a number of areas, are not more rapidly employed within the educational system? Should not education be a nation's top priority?

Today we are on the threshold of a new era. Peace is knocking on the door, accompanied by a growing sense of equality and democracy. At the same time, strong emphasis is being placed on the development of scientific and hi-tech fields in Israel. Within this climate, the attitudes of women and their roles, as well as their contributions to the future society of the twenty-first century will gain importance in the educational system. The knowledge and abilities of girls and women will have to be promoted. Gender inequality is a waste of precious resources and potential and not in keeping with the declared values of a democratic Israel. There is, therefore, no doubt that the educational system must and can be the motor of change of our society. New educational attitudes towards both sexes will allow long-term growth as well as broader conceptions of greater equality in society as a whole.

The Intervention Model of Gender Equality for Student Teachers in Higher Education

The idea that gender equality must be a part of the various programmes which train teachers in colleges, seminars and universities, was first conceived by a group of lecturers who were dedicated to this cause. Hence, a "forum for education of gender equality" was founded within the College of Seminar HaKibbutzim. This is composed of both male and female teachers, some of whom give courses which touch directly upon questions of gender difference. In addition, teachers who were active promoters of gender equality in all kinds of frameworks were persuaded to join the initiative. Some are teachers who either focus on gender equality as the main topic of their courses, or teach the possible influences of gender inequality in classes dealing with subjects such as Literature, Philosophy, Mathematics, Languages and Social Studies.

The members of the forum believe that the College of Seminar HaKibbutzim, which trains and instils within our future teachers the values of humanity and democracy, must be a leading force in the promotion of gender equality in society, thus it is essential to implement the principles stated. In this way, gender equality must be conceived of as one of the key objectives of education, as well as a vital dimension in all college and university educational programmes.

The main objective of the forum is to create intervention programmes which will allow the student to acquire:

i)   awareness of personal conceptions and attitudes regarding gender equality;
ii) a deeper comprehension and knowledge in topics of gender inequality, the reasons for its existence, and the losses and damages that it causes;
iii) teaching skills in this area.

Intervention Programmes Promoting Change in Teacher Training

1. **The Compilation of a Group of Courses Serving as a Focal Area in Education for Equality**
    Each course addresses a different issue of gender equality from a specific angle. These courses are important because

they challenge the subject of inequality from a number of points of view - sociological, psychological, political, literary, as well as from that of human sexuality itself.

This collection of courses can include additional areas. A student who takes all of the courses, or at least the basic ones, is constantly reinforced and supported in the process of change he/she is experiencing, since he/she is learning the subject from different aspects and points of view presented by the different lecturers. He/she learns that the lack of equality is a very complex social reality and is reflected in all areas of our life. Such an approach clarifies to the student the reasons and implications of gender inequality in society, while enhancing their awareness of this subject.

A student who takes all of the courses (or at least 4 basic ones), will become a "professional" as well as an "agent of change" in the school in which he/she is located. It is his/her responsibility to organize seminars for the other teachers on the subject of equality and promote this issue among students and parents. In addition, he/she is responsible for integrating the idea of gender equality within the school.

The participants in this course will also be part of a support group, acting as a tool that encourages the process of change. Furthermore, in higher education, they are expected to participate in the established seminars on the topic of equality, so as to gain both national and international knowledge.

2. **The Establishment of Centres for the Study of Gender Equality, which will include:**
    i)   a library that will be used as a research centre on the subject;
    ii) initiative and encouragement of research and the planning of follow-up studies for the intervention programmes (an example is that which is part of doctoral research);

iii)   constructing seminar programmes for active teachers;
iv)   writing educational programmes;
v)   distributing information to all the college systems.

3. **Inclusion of the Subject of Equality in the Mandatory Courses Given in the College**
    All year-long courses in subjects such as Sociology, Psychology, Literature,Mathematics and so on will integrate within their syllabuses a number of lectures that are relevant to the subject.

4. **Introducing Elective Courses in Additional Subjects Related to Gender Equality**
    These permit a deeper knowledge of the subject of gender equality and lead to an overall insight for students.

The central message of the forum is that gender inequality is a waste of resources and potential and must be tackled at all levels.

Figure 1

A Model to Promote Sensitization regarding Gender Equality within the Educational System

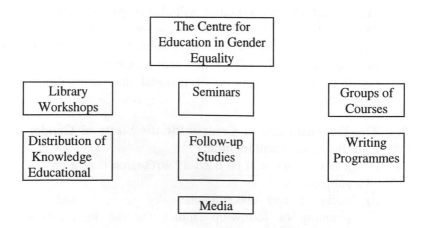

Additional Subjects Addressed in the Programme
a) Why did I choose Teaching as a Profession?

Although a number of men and women choose the occupation of teaching for idealistic reasons and because of their belief in the importance of education, unfortunately, the majority of the women appear to be motivated by other forces. Therefore, it is imperative to understand the reasons why people choose teaching when providing gender equality instruction for young teachers in colleges. A number of studies have been done which clarify the motives behind the choice of a profession. The School of Education at Bar-Ilan, Carmeli (1993) studied the relationship between background variables, the need for social approval, attitudes towards motherhood and the femininity or masculinity of the chosen profession. She checked the relationship between background variables such as a woman's education, parents' education, husband's education, parents' origin, religious commitment and family status, and the level of masculinity or femininity of the subject's chosen occupation. The key variables were:

1. the woman's need for social approval;
2. her attitudes towards motherhood.

Figure 2
The Relationship Between Background and Mediating Variables of Attitudes Towards Motherhood and the Need for Social Approval and Their Influence on the Choice of Occupation

Background Variables

The woman's level of education - Husband's education - Family status	Parent's education - Origin of parents - Attitude to religion

Need for Social Approval	AttitudesTowards Motherhood

Occupational Choice

Feminine Occupation - Teacher - Nurse - Secretary	Masculine Occupation - Engineer - Company Manager - Lawyer

Extracted from: Carmeli, Michal, M.A. Thesis, Bar-Ilan, 1993

The sample included women whose occupations were masculine or feminine, as well as women who were married with children and unmarried. The findings indicate that:

i)   a strong need for social approval and conservative attitudes towards motherhood are significantly related to occupations that are considered as typically feminine, such as teaching;

ii) the more religious the woman, the greater her need for social approval; in addition, her attitudes towards motherhood appear to be very conservative. Consequently, her tendency to work in classical occupations, such as teaching, is greater than among non-religious women;

iii) married women from the Middle East with a number of children expressed more conservative attitudes towards motherhood, and worked in more feminine occupations, such as teaching, compared to their unmarried Western counterparts;

iv) the more educated the woman, the more liberal her attitudes are towards motherhood, and the greater her tendency to work in masculine occupations, as opposed to feminine ones;

v)   likewise, highly educated husbands often had wives with very liberal attitudes towards motherhood and a greater tendency to work in traditionally masculine occupations.

The rationale for the choice of a feminine profession, such as teaching, demonstrates the social and cultural pressures which are placed on women. As a result, their motivation in the occupational area is usually lowered. A woman who chooses a masculine occupation, which requires considerable commitment and devotion, breaks the code of social norms and may expose herself to a situation of social disapproval. Hence, the feminine occupation represents a compromise which fulfils the expectations of her social environment, and the demands of her role as the more responsible parent and housekeeper. Here, one can see that women have a great need to receive social approval for their choice of occupation, to obtain positive social recognition, and to please the family entourage (mother-in-law, husband, children, mother and neighbours), while ignoring their own needs.

There is also of course a relationship between this and conservative attitudes towards motherhood. Together, these two factors together steer the woman to the occupation of teaching.

The major conclusion of the reviewed studies is the need to invest a greater amount of resources in equal socialization, which must begin at a very early age, in order to release our young ones from the more traditional conceptions of gender roles. By doing this, the realization of girls' abilities and potential which are not expressed in their occupational roles and choices will be achieved.

b) **Teachers as Leaders and Role Models: Leadership Workshop for Teachers**
An additional way to promote education in gender equality is to work on self-awareness with the teachers themselves - both their place in the organizational hierarchy at their work-place, and the development of their leadership skills. Such increased self-awareness and skills will allow them to advance into positions of power and decision-making within their working environment. The aim is that the teachers (most often women) will act as role models. This will be the case not only in their classroom teaching, but also with regard to their ability to take advantage of the equal opportunities existing within the organization, which will then allow the expression of their own personal abilities and potential. For this reason, a seminar for educational leadership within the educational system was developed.

Entitled[2] "Coping with the Role of Leadership while Staying Alive," its goal is to sensitize teachers within the educational system to their own personal strengths and abilities to contribute, at high levels of decision-making, to their organizations. In this way, they will not only be empowered within their professional context, but they will also be able to advance into positions of authority within the Teachers' Union. It is important to note that in Israel, there are approximately 100,000 teachers, 90% of whom are women. In spite of this, the head of the Union is a man, and he is surrounded by an executive committee which is mainly male in composition.

In order to foster educational leadership, 100 women were selected as having exceptional potential within the system. They came from all over the country to participate in a two-day study programme which first focused on the distribution of knowledge and information via various research studies, and addressed the possible reasons for the lack of equality in the educational system in Israel. It also analysed the implications of this inequality for the status of men and women in the society at the macro level which included, inter alia, the labour market, the economy, politics and the media.

The second part of the study programme was a workshop with a micro-level focus. Each one of the participants examined her personal attitudes towards equality, her bases of power, and the motives, fears and barriers, which appear to determine her behavioural patterns. For example, women who were heard to say such things as: "I always do all of the work and yet remain the Vice-Principal, I am afraid to be at the top of the pyramid, to be the Principal, I have been socialised to give in, to be subservient." Later on in the day, a simulation experiment took place during which the participants divided into groups and competed in relevant leadership tasks. Each group represented a party running in the elections for the National Teachers' Union. They had to elect a chairwoman, present a platform with innovative ideas about the educational system, choose a name for the party, prepare a campaign including an election speech delivered in front of all of the teachers in the country, slogans, jingles, explanatory pamphlets for distribution and a media plan. All of this was to be carried out within a limited budget. The simulations themselves were filmed on a closed-circuit television and were then shown to each of the competing parties, along with an analysis of the leadership situation. This included a map-reading of power relations within the group ("why didn't I take the role of the leader, why did I give it up in the beginning?"), understanding the rules of the game, the use of force in personal and group decision-making and the checking of the self in three roles: teacher, politically active and leader. In the future, additional study days will be offered to ensure that this training in leadership skills receives further attention.

c)   **Retraining of Senior Teachers in Educational Systems**
In addition to training young teachers in higher education, for their future role, there is a need to retrain senior teachers who have already worked within the system for many years. In order to achieve this purpose, the Minister of Education, initiated gender equality programmes at both local and national levels. The programmes were run by the Israel Women's' Network, whose aim is to promote equal status for women in Israeli society.

A large part of the program is intended to train group facilitators in the area of equal opportunities in education within a two-year framework. The entry requirement for the training course is at least an undergraduate degree in both education and group facilitation as well as experience in these fields. Participants are expected to work with the teachers, supervisors, counsellors and principals in workshops on the subject of gender equality. This is not to be treated as a separate issue, but rather the idea of mainstreaming the gender dimension into every subject taught in the school is given strong emphasis. In addition, facilitators of parent groups are also trained to include gender equality in their retraining programmes. Thus, the entire system will be oriented towards gender equality, beginning with teachers of 4 year-old children and all the way through to university level. Furthermore, training programmes in technology for girls are being established and receive additional resources and specially trained teachers.

In September 1995, all nurseries with children from the age of 4 upwards received learning materials that deal with the subject of gender equality.[3] Every teacher will be trained and guided in how to work with these. The aim is that girls, like boys, will realize their full potential, that more girls will take science disciplines and that they will enter into the top echelons of the labour market. In this way, more women will have access to positions of power and the tools of empowerment and advancement will be in their hands.

Gender Issues and the University Curriculum

There is no doubt that UNESCO's programmes in higher education and the policies and aims of Israel in this area are in harmony. Higher education is considered to be one major component of progress, peace and stability in our region. However, in reality, the Israeli universities still do not place enough importance on the issue of gender equality. As a result, resources are not invested in subjects that are related to gender issues and research institutions are not being established or given adequate support. What we see are courses addressing gender equality, which are not the outcome of a general university policy, but which are the result of the initiative of mostly female lecturers who firmly believe in this principle and who see to it personally that such courses are offered. Since the number of the courses is small and not mandatory, most of the students - except for those in the teacher training programmes - are not exposed to the issues of gender equality, and therefore they enter both the frameworks of the family and work force with traditional perceptions which prevent women from realizing their potential. It is in this way that the lack of equality is perpetuated. To this, we must add the fact that the role model for university lecturers is masculine and that most of the top positions are held by men - only 13% of the academic faculty with tenure are women (Toren, 1993) and only 1 out of 8 professors is a women (Israel Women's Network, 1995). Thus, it may be concluded that the university, which should in fact be the leader and model of social change, is actually a fortress maintaining traditional perceptions and ideologies.

Conclusion

The aim of higher education is to enable both sexes to realize their full potential, so that integration may be achieved in key areas of society, such as education, politics, the economy and the media. The long-term objective is to advance the goals of Israeli society in general. The fact that women remain absent in higher education in many fields blocks their advancement into prestigious and influential positions in society. This has particularly serious consequences for Science, Technology and the professions requiring qualifications in Economics and Business. Equal opportunities in education constitute a major factor for social change, equality and democracy in Israeli society and so must be available to both sexes throughout their life - from an early age, during the period of higher education and beyond - as an integral part of the life-long learning process.

Bibliography

AAUW Report. "How Schools Short Change Girls." Wellesley College Centre for Research on Women. AAUW Education Foundation, Washington, D.C, 1992.

Amit, M., Moshevitz-Hadar, N. "Differences Between Boys and Girls in the Attributions of Reasons for Success and Failure in Mathematics." *Megamot*, 32 (3), 361-371, (Hebrew), 1989.

Amit, M.. Unpublished Research, 1993.

Avrahami, E.J. "Latent Messages - Gender Interactions in Israeli Schools." Doctoral Dissertation presented at London University, England, 1993.

Ayalon, C.H. "The Coming of the Future: Economic Aspects of Boys' and Girls' Vocational Aspirations." *Megamot*, 31 (2), 133-151, (Hebrew), 1988.

Baker, D. "Sex Differences in Classroom Interactions in Secondary School." *Journal of Classroom Interaction*, 22. 216-218, 1986.

Ben Tzvi-Mayer, S. "The Daughter in Formal Education." *Iunim BeChinuch*, 22, 12, 107-144. (Hebrew), 1976.

Ben Tzvi-Mayer, S. "Masculine and Feminine Figures in Mathematic Problems." *Hachinuch*, A-B. (Hebrew), 1979.

Ben Tzvi-Mayer, S., Ben Zeev, S., & Avrahami, E.J. "Trapped in Pink and Light Blue: Girls and Boys in the Eyes of Society." (Pamphlet for the teacher and the student), *Oranim*, Israel. (Hebrew), 1985.

Ben Tzvi-Mayer, S., Hertz-Lazarowitz, R., & Safir, M. "Teachers and Teacher Trainees on the Classification of Boys and Girls as Prominent Students". *Iunim BeChinuch,* 53 (53), 71-78. (Hebrew), 1990.

Ben Tzvi-Mayer, S. "Teaching Girls to be Women in Israeli Jewish Schools". In B. Swirski and B.M. Safir (eds.). *Calling the Equality Bluff: Women in Israel,* Pergamon Press, USA, 1991.

Chasidov, D. *"Achievements in Mathematics with Computer Assistance in Two Study Environments."* M.A. Thesis, Haifa University, Israel, 1995.

Ephroni, L. "Men and Women in the Civil Service in Israel." Jerusalem: The Advisor of the Status of Women in the Offices of the Prime Minister, 1990.

Hertz-Lazarowitz, R. "Coeducation as a Means to Creating a Democratic Climate in the Classroom." In S. Zdekiouhu (ed.) *Climate in the Classroom - Meaning and Practice*, Jerusalem: The Ministry of Education and Culture, Beit Berl, p. 129-157. (Hebrew), 1988.

Hertz-Lazarowitz, R., & Chadell, B. *Cooperative Learning,* Haifa: Haifa University, 1992.

Herzog, H. "Realistic Women - Women in the Local Politics of Israel." Jerusalem: The Jerusalem Institute of Research, 1994.

Lee, V. "Sexism in Single Sex and Co-educational Secondary School Classrooms." Paper presented at the American Sociology Association, Cincinnati, August, 1991.

Lemish, D., & Tidhar, C.H. "The Silenced Majority: Women in Israel 1988 Television Election Campaign." *Women and Language*, XIV (1), 13-21, 1990.

Lieblich, A. "Sex Differences in Intelligence Test Performances of Jewish and Arab School Children in Israel." In M.P. Safir, M.S. Imednick, D. Izraeli & J. Bernard (eds.). *Women's Worlds: From the New Scholarship*. New York: Praeger Publications, 1985..

Malkiel, Z., Phredkin, N., & Kleinman "The Attitude Towards the Male and Female in Textbooks." The Ministry of Education and Culture, the Branch for Educational Programs, Israel. (Hebrew), 1987.

Maller, T. "The Stereotypical Sexual Validity in Textbooks in the Public School System in Israel." HaChinuch Vesvivo, Annual of the College of the Seminar HaKibbutzim, p. 86-100, 1991..

Plissler, Y. (ed.) "Women in Israel - Information, Data and Interpretation". Jerusalem: The Israeli Women's Network, 1995.

Sadker, D., & Sadker, M. "Is the Classroom OK?" *Phidelta Kap ppan*, 55, 358- 367, 1985.

Safir, M. "The Effects of Nature or of Nurture in Sex Differences in Intellectual Functioning: Israeli Findings." *Sex Roles*, 14, 581-590, 1986.

Safir, M., Hertz-Lazarowitz, R., Ben Tzvi-Mayer, S., & Kupermintz, H. "Prominence of Girls and Boys in the Classrooms: School Children's Perceptions." *Sex Roles*, 27 (9/10), 353-439, 1992.

Shachar, R. "Is the Educational System Perpetuating Gender Inequality"? In R. Shachar & J. Avrahami (eds.), 1993. *Equal Opportunities for Boys and Girls in the Educational System.* The Israeli Women Network, Jerusalem, 1993..

"The Influence of Gender Role Socialization on Student Perceptions." State of Michigan, Department of Education, Office of Set Equity in Education, June, 1990.

The Statistical Annual of Israel. 1994.

"Tomorrow 98." A report by the Committee of Higher Education in Technological Sciences (the Harrari Committee). The Ministry of Education and Culture, Israel. (Hebrew).

Toren, N. "Women and Men in the Faculty of the Hebrew University of Jerusalem, 1983-1993." Annual Report. (Hebrew), 1993.

Zeidman, A., Loker, A., & Rom, J. "The 'NAALE' Programme, an Intervention Program to Raise the Number of Female Students in the Studies of Technology at an Increased Level at the Hadera High School." *'AL' A, Alon Lemore Lematimatica*, March (10). (Hebrew), 1992.

Notes

1. Extracted from the information pamphlet: *Women in Israel - Information, Data and Interpretation* Published by the Israel Women's Network, 1995.
2. See Levin (1995, Development and Training Programs in Leadership in the Educational System, The Israel Women's Network, Jerusalem, Israel.
3. See Appendix 1

Notes on the Contributors

Sheryl Bond is professor of Higher Education at Queen's University, Canada and formerly directed the Centre for Higher Education Research and Development (CHERD) at the University of Manitoba.

Robyn Dormer lectures in Chemistry at the University of Auckland, New Zealand and also runs her own consultancy firm.

Maria Teresa Gallego is professor of Political Science at the Universidad Autónoma de Madrid, Spain; **Otilia Mó** is professor of Chemical Physics and director of the Institute for Women's Studies in the same institution.

Henrietta Mensa-Bonsu is a barrister and senior lecturer in the Faculty of Law at the University of Ghana, Legon.

Sandra Levison M. D., professor and Associate Chair of Medicine, and **Katherine Sherif M. D**. teach at the Medical College of Pennsylvania and Hahnemann University, Philadelphia, USA.

Margaret Gardner, Pro-Vice-Chancellor (Equity) at Griffith University, Australia, is a professor in the Commerce and Administration Faculty.

Zhizhen Gui is a professor and principal of the China College for Women Administrators, Beijing, People's Republic of China

Anne Holden Rønning is associate professor of English at the University of Bergen, Norway

Maria Inacia d'Avila Neto is director of the Institute of Psychology at the Universidade Federal de Rio de Janeiro, Brazil; she co-ordinates the UNESCO Chair in Sustainable Development at that institution.

Sanáa Osseiran is an expert in Political Science and the UNESCO representative of the International Peace Research Association (IPRA).

Ralitsa Muharska, a professor of English, directs the Women's Studies Programme at the St Kliment Ochrid University, Sofia, Bulgaria.

Mouna Samman, an expert in Demography and a former university professor, now works in the UNESCO Programme for Environmental and Population Development

Rina Shachar is a specialist in teacher training and lectures in this field at Bar-Ilan University, Israel.

Mary-Louise Kearney lectured at the Université de Paris II and is now with the Division of Higher Education of UNESCO.